P9-CAN-041

The
Romance Writer's Handbook

The
Romance
Writer's
Handbook

by

Rebecca Vinyard

THE WRITER BOOKS

The Writer Books is an imprint of Kalmbach Trade Press, a division of Kalmbach Publishing Co. These books are distributed to the book trade by Watson-Guptill.

For all other inquiries, including individual orders or details on special quantity discounts for groups or conferences, contact:

Kalmbach Publishing Co.
21027 Crossroads Circle
Waukesha, WI 53187
(800) 533-6644

Visit our website at http://writermag.com
Secure online ordering available

For feedback on this or any other title by The Writer Books, contact us at this e-mail address: writerbooks@kalmbach.com.

© 2004 Rebecca Vinyard. All rights reserved. This book may not be reproduced in part or in whole without written permission of the publisher, except in the case of brief quotations used in reviews.

Printed in Canada

03 04 05 06 07 08 09 10 11 12   10 9 8 7 6 5 4 3 2 1

Publisher's Cataloging-in-Publication

    Vinyard, Rebecca.
       The romance writer's handbook / by Rebecca Vinyard.
       p. cm.
       Includes bibliographical references and index.
       ISBN 0-87116-204-0

       1. Love stories--Authorship--Handbooks, manuals, etc.
    I. Title

    PN3377.5.L68V56 2004   808.3'85
                      QBI03-200794
Text design by Mighty Media, Minneapolis
Cover design by Lisa Bergman
Illustration by Kellie Jaeger

ACKNOWLEDGMENTS

This book would not have been possible without the participation and gracious cooperation of all of the contributing authors. To them, my most heartfelt thanks.

I would also like to thank those people who generously took the time to give interviews; authors Suzanne Brockmann, Judy Christenberry, Connie Flynn, Lorraine Heath, Susan Elizabeth Phillips, and Kathleen Sutcliffe; editors Lucia Macro (Avon Books), Leslie Wainger (Harlequin, New York), and Dick Claassen (Awe-Struck E-Books); agents Evan M. Fogelman (Fogelman Literary Agency) and Natasha Kern (Natasha Kern Agency); and Charis Calhoon (Romance Writers of America).

A special thank you to Philip Martin from The Writer Books for suggesting I compile this book in the first place.

And a big thank you to Jack, Nicole, Bob, Mollie, Teresa, and the Dallas Area Romance Authors for always being there when I need them. May all of your dreams come true.

6743

CONTENTS

IF YOU ARE HOLDING THIS BOOK in your hot little hands, then you're probably considering becoming a romance writer. Or perhaps, you already *are* a romance writer and are simply looking for support, inspiration, and information.

Either way, sit down, relax, kick your shoes off. You've come to the right place.

When I finished writing my first romance, I didn't have a clue what to do next. I read various writing magazines and how-to books looking for answers, but couldn't find anything specifically related to the romance market. I sent out a flood of query letters to editors and agents, only to get a flood of rejections in return.

I knew I must be doing something wrong, but I didn't know where to find help. And then one day, I found it—on the Internet!

Now this was over ten years ago when the Internet was a vastly different place. Yahoo was in its infancy and there were few search engines. Most sites and message boards were accessible via colleges or major Internet servers such as AOL and Prodigy.

So it felt like a miracle when I discovered a romance writers board on Prodigy.

We shared information on research sources and changes in the romance market. We discussed various ways to improve our writing techniques and set up online critique groups. And I learned about this wonderful organization for romance writers called the Romance Writers of America (RWA).

As romance authors, we gave each other unconditional support. Authors from other genres thought we were all nuts. The board manager, a multi-published author, once asked us, "Why are you helping the competition?"

Our reply was something along the lines of "Because we can."

That's the amazing thing about romance writers. Their hearts are as big as those of their heroes and heroines. I felt I owed these authors something in return for their help. I elected to "pass it on." I started a little website on Prodigy with links to various research and romance related websites and called it Romance Central.

Over the years, Romance Central grew into a rather large website that includes a romance writers workshop with dozens of articles on writing, an online critique group, a message board, and book reviews.

This experience has taught me one thing—writers have an endless supply of questions. I've been asked everything from how to grow an idea into a story to what is the best way to promote a book online.

Which brings us to this book you're holding in your hot little hands. *The Romance Writer's Handbook* provides information for romance writers in all stages of their careers. In this book, you'll find articles on writing, critiquing, contests, and book promotion, as well as submission guidelines and interviews with authors, editors, and agents.

The path to publication is different for every writer. But my hope is, with this book in hand, your journey will be swift and successful.

So let's get started, shall we?

Section 1

For Beginners

CHAPTER 1

Advice for
the New Writer

I N THE LAST WEEK, I received three e-mails that all had one thing in common. They were from beginning writers who didn't know where or how to *begin*. Each had oodles of story ideas. Their characters carried on conversations in their heads. They all had the desire to write, but didn't have a clue how to get started.

I felt sorry for them. They felt so alone, as if something was wrong with them for having the ideas, the character conversations—the desire to be writers. This article is for all of you who find yourself in that state—to let you know you are not alone. And probably not crazy either.

Although to be honest, I've always thought you *had* to be a bit nuts to want to be a writer in the first place.

So this one's for all you wannabe writers. I hope you'll find the advice and encouragement you need to face that ominous blank page.

First, let's talk about ideas. Some writers tell me they get ideas all the time, but don't know what to do with them. If you fall into this category, count yourself lucky. I wouldn't go moaning about this problem in the presence of someone experiencing writer's block. Especially since this is one of the easiest problems to fix.

Ready for the magic answer?

Write down your ideas!

Well, you might be thinking, how obvious can she get? Sometimes the obvious eludes us though, especially if you are a wannabe writer experiencing blank-page fright for the first time. Allow me to introduce you to the concept of pre-writing.

Pre-Writing

What is pre-writing? Pre-writing is the writing you do *before* you start to work on your story. Pre-writing becomes a sort of blueprint from which you can begin to build your novel.

I am one of those lucky writers who finds ideas everywhere. Guess what I do with them? *I write them down.* Nothing fancy, because the only person who will ever see these story notes is me. I don't have to worry about grammar. I don't have to worry about punctuation or manuscript format or picking the right word. All I have to do is *write*.

That's the beauty of pre-writing; at this point you are only writing for you. There's no pressure, just the joy of getting that idea out of your head and onto a page.

So, try doing that first . . . and guess what, wannabe writer? You're writing!

Now that you have that idea down, let's talk about those characters rattling around in your head. Where are they from? What do they want? What do they look like? Give your imaginary people an interview and *write down* their answers.

Again, this is pre-writing. Before you attempt page one of your manuscript, your characters should be old friends. You should know everything about them, more than your readers will ever know.

If you *are* hearing those characters, count yourself lucky. Not every writer does. (For those of us who do have conversations with our characters, there is nothing more frustrating than a character that won't talk. But sometimes talking to them is even more frustrating, because they don't always want to go along with our neatly plotted scenarios. So yes, Virginia, sometimes you can have too much of a good thing.)

Okay, so you've written out your story idea and you know your characters. Are you finished pre-writing your story yet?

Plotting

Nope, let's talk plotting now. Here's the thing: not every writer plots a story the same way. Some work strictly from outlines. Some write by the seat of their pants—I'm in this category most of the time. But I usually have a basic idea of where I want to go and how to get there.

So I write the plot down as far as I know it. What my characters want, the external and internal conflicts facing them, maybe a snatch of a conversation here and there. I know the moment of truth and how it all ends.

So more or less, by the time I'm done with pre-writing, I have also developed a basic plot structure. Now, whether or not I stick to that structure depends on what happens while I'm actually writing the story in earnest.

This method may or may not work for you. That's part of the joy of writing. It's a different experience for everyone, because each writer is different.

Research

Now are we done pre-writing? Sorry, but no. Have you done your research? Research is essential for almost any story. Look at your story's setting—do you know all there is to know about the place? And how about your characters?—do you know all about their occupations and hobbies? Look over your notes and think about the things you'll need to know. Then go look them up. And for goodness sakes, *write them down*.

When you've done all this, maybe you're finished pre-writing.

I say maybe, because who knows? Maybe you will start writing the story . . . and then realize you don't know what a common woman wore in 16th-century Scotland. Maybe your character reveals something about herself you didn't know, so you need to explore that side of herself in your notes. Or maybe your plot changes. Whatever the case, you'll probably want to return to your notes often. I usually write with my file of notes close at hand, just in case I need to refer to them. Or add to them as the case may be.

Anyway, let's say you're done prewriting. It's time to start working on your story. Where do you begin?

Starting to Write

How about by writing something like . . . *Chapter One*?

You have to start somewhere. So why not start at the beginning. Even with *Chapter One* written at the top, it's still the same blank page staring back at you. But hopefully, all the pre-writing you did will give you the courage to tackle all that whiteness and plunge ahead.

You're eager and ready. You start writing . . . and one page flows after another.

But let's say it doesn't. Perhaps you've pre-written enough to fill a hundred pages, but still don't know how to begin.

Getting in Shape

Maybe the problem isn't your story. Maybe, my dear wannabe writer, it's you. Maybe you need to get your writing muscles in shape. A healthy dose of confidence wouldn't hurt either.

My mom-in-law's first gift to me was a wonderful book called *Writing Down the Bones* by Natalie Goldberg. In this book, Natalie compares writing to distance running. Just as you shouldn't take on a marathon run without getting your body into shape, you shouldn't start a novel without toning up your writing muscles.

If you want to be a writer, you need to start writing on a regular schedule, preferably every day. It should become part of your routine. Can't write that first page? Then write something else. Try an article ... like this one (writing about your own writing habits can be revealing.)

Or how about a poem?

Too ambitious? Then try a letter to a friend. Or maybe a simple journal entry? All involve the act of writing. By doing any of them *every day*, you are getting those writing muscles in shape.

Jump-Starts

Here's something that usually jump-starts me. Try writing via free association, or stream of consciousness. If you can touch-type, close your eyes and type out whatever comes to mind. Can't touch-type? Then pick up a paper and pen and try writing that way. You might be surprised at what you have going on up there.

I use this method to work out problems when I can't think of solutions. Or sometimes, I use it just to get in touch with what I'm really feeling. Try it. Trust me, this one works. Not only will you exercise your writing muscles, you'll get to know yourself a little better too.

Confidence-Building

Besides building writing muscles, you need to build confidence. Writers by nature are an insecure lot. It comes with the territory. So ask yourself, what can I do to build confidence in my writing?

How about joining a writing group? The old cliché about misery loving company is definitely true for most writers. Surround yourself with people who also know what it's like to face that blasted blank page; it will help boost your confidence and energize your desire to write.

I can hear some of you moaning now . . . but I'm not really a writer yet! What could I possibly have to say to a writers' group? Easy. Just ask *them* about what they're working on. Trust me, you'll get an earful. When asked about yourself, be honest. You'll be amazed at how encouraging other writers can be, particularly romance writers.

Romance Writers of America has chapters all across the country, including special-interest and online groups. These chapters offer speakers who will tell you how to improve your writing or inspire you to keep trying. And when you're ready, they can help you with the business of selling your work too. Don't be shy, wannabe writer. Get out there and start sharing your misery. A writers' group can turn your frown upside down in no time.

Eventually, you're going to want someone to read what you're working on. A critique group can be helpful. It might take a while to find a group that works for you, but it is well worth the effort. Once you find the right group, they can give you valuable feedback, becoming a sounding board for your ideas.

In the end though, it's all up to *you*, wannabe writer. You say you have the desire to tell a story. There's only one way you can do that.

Write it down.

Because that's what a writer does . . . write.

CHAPTER 2

The Idea Garden

MARY, MARY, QUITE CONTRARY. . . how do your ideas grow? Authors are frequently asked in interviews, "Where do you get your ideas?" Usually, they have a pat answer to rattle off (it beats letting out an exasperated groan.) But I'm guessing that nine times out of ten, it isn't the whole truth.

Now I'm not saying they're liars, although having a vivid imagination is definitely a plus for any writer. Especially when you apply that imagination to the creation of new ideas.

No, what I mean is this: Ideas are one of life's little intangibles. For some of us, nothing we think of seems original. So we wonder, what do these authors know that we don't? They must have some secret store, some magical resource they can tap into anytime they want. Right?

I'm very sorry to tell you this, but there are no secret stores or magical trees. The creation and development of ideas is difficult to describe. There is no single method authors use to generate new and original concepts. Luckily, we're all capable of creating fresh story ideas. The trick is being able to recognize a concept and make it bloom.

I like to think of story ideas as flowers. You have to grow them yourself. Some ideas begin as tiny seeds. It takes time and nurturing before they grow into stories. Some ideas arrive in full bloom, ready to be written. Some are even transplanted ideas. This happens when another writer is generous enough to pass along few seedlings. But don't count on that. If you're going to be a writer, you need to learn how to grow your own ideas.

Maybe it will help if I take you on a tour of my idea garden. Please keep in mind that my way of growing stories is not the only way. Each writer has a process that works for him or her. The trick is figuring out what works for you.

First, let's take a look at the idea for this article. Can you guess how I thought of it? Gardening. That's right, gardening. As I planted seeds in my front yard this weekend, I realized gardening is a lot like writing. A story idea is a like a seed. Editing is like digging out weeds. Take the analogies all the way to their logical end and I guess your prettiest blossoms will end up in a flower shop some day.

The point is: I started by making an association (i.e., gardening is like writing). From that seed, the idea for this article began to grow. How did I know I needed this seed? Ah, now there's a good question. The opening paragraph has the answer. Authors are frequently asked where they get their ideas. So when the idea came, I knew there was a need for it.

This is why writers are told to study the market. Read to get a feel for what is needed. If you are writing category romance, read as much as you can of your targeted line. If your goal is single-title romance, then read widely to figure out which houses might be most receptive to your story.

I'm not saying to write with your eye on sales. It's always best to write what is in your heart. Writing with dollar signs in your eyes takes all the joy out of it. Instead, think of reading as the soil in your idea garden's flower bed. If you don't study the market, you won't know what kind of ideas you need.

Let's get back to associations. Have you ever looked at a stranger and made up a story about them in your head? That's an idea based on an association. Ideas can come from anywhere and everywhere—reading the newspaper, watching a movie, or visiting with your friends. Even gardening.

So keep your eyes open. Take everything you experience and use your experiences to generate new ideas.

Maybe you have a great idea for a story, but you can't figure out how to make it grow. You need to nurture it, just as you would any seedling. Again, reading can help. If you research everything that has to do with your idea, it can inspire new possibilities for that little sprout and help it grow.

Can't find the answer in books? Then maybe you need to get out there and live it. Want to write about hot air balloons? Go take a balloon ride. Watch a hot-air balloon race. Talk to balloonists. You'll learn more this way than from simple research. You can now write about how it feels to be way up in the air. You'll know the sights, the scents, and the sounds, because you've been there (or talked with others who have)!

Story notes

In reality, my "idea garden" consists of story notes stored on my computer. These story ideas are in various stages of growth. Some are still little seeds; some are already blooming. Whenever I have a flash of inspiration about a specific story, I add it to the notes. Sort of like watering the seed.

By the time I finish with my current project, I usually know which story comes next. It's the one with the biggest and brightest blooms, just begging to be picked. I can "see" and "hear" the characters. The plot rolls along like so many stepping-stones. The conflict and theme are crystal clear. All these story elements grow as I nurture the initial idea along.

Some ideas grow quickly. For instance, my next project is actually my latest idea. This one came to me in full bloom. I've lived some of it myself, and I've read about the rest. I feel I "know" the characters. I've been constantly adding to this story's notes; already the file surpasses all the others. This story is ready. But it has to wait until I finish the one I'm working on first!

Some of my story ideas have been in the seedling stage for years. Maybe I'll never write them. Then again, maybe I will. When I'm blocked on my current manuscript, I often find it helpful to take a walk through my idea garden. I add a bit here. Pinch off a bit there. It frees my mind to make associations. And associations are the roots of many ideas.

So, dear writer, how does your idea garden grow?

Not with silver bells and cockleshells. It's by writing what you know.

Yes, that's an old writer's saw, but think of it as meaning writing what you know is *ready* to be written.

You're the Mistress Mary of your idea garden. It's up to you to decide how and when your ideas grow into stories.

CHAPTER 3

Stuck in the Starting Gate

I RECENTLY STARTED WORK on a new story. Oh, I was *sooo* eager to start on this one. I felt it was my best idea yet. I had done some research. The setting and characters were vivid in my mind. I could "hear" the characters' voices. I even had an outline of sorts. I had it all.

I was *ready* to write this story. So I started. I wrote a chapter. I showed it to my critique group and was advised to dump the first three scenes.

I did. And then . . . I promptly became stuck. I didn't have a clue where to go from there. *Sigh!!*

Now, mind you, I've had minor tangles with writer's block before. Never at the start of the story though. I've always written the first three chapters in overdrive. Then I settle down to a calmer pace, building from the set-up.

Not this time. I'd open up the story's file and stare the blank monitor, willing the words to show up. They didn't.

Dialogue—whole scenes—flashed through my head, at all hours of the day and night . . . but nothing useful for the opening chapters. It was great stuff for later scenes, but I had to get there first.

I was good and stuck in the starting gate and couldn't find a way to blow that gate open.

For some people, this would not be a problem. Many non-linear writers compose scenes in chunks, then stitch them together later into a chronological order. I can't work that way. I'm a linear thinker; I have to go in a straight line from point A to point B. I have to put each brick in place as I go, leaving no gaps in the yellow brick road behind me.

But this road was going nowhere. I needed help! So I wrote a few e-mails and called a few writer friends, asking for advice. Some said I should put back the scenes I took out and see if that helped. Others said I should write a *real* outline. Others said, scrap everything and start over.

All good advice. I tried it all, too. I put back the scenes, but they still weren't working. I tried to write a real outline. You'd think a linear writer wouldn't dare set foot in the starting gate without one, but in my case, outlines are usually a waste of time. My characters tend to haul me off in other directions. I usually outline only the next three to five chapters. And even then, I rarely stick to the road map.

I got more and more frustrated. Putting the scenes back didn't help. Outlining didn't help. The only option left (shudder) was to scrap everything and start over. Or (shudder, shudder) just forget the whole thing.

I decided what I needed to do was step back and *analyze* my problem. Here's what I came up with:

I have a great story idea. I'm really dying to write it.

But there's an old saying, haste makes waste.

I certainly was being hasty. What had I overlooked?

Research is the Backbone

The backbone of every story is research.

Bing! Maybe I should go through my research again. Out came my notes, off I went to the library, and on I went to surf the Internet. But this time, I didn't simply focus on the main subject idea for my story. I looked up information on the settings too—plus information on my characters' careers, hobbies, and interests. These were the missing bricks in my yellow brick road.

With historicals, you *have* to do research. There's no way around it. I started my career writing historicals, and I loved the research process. Often, those dry tomes of "what, when, where, and why" have gems of story ideas lurking inside, semi-precious stones that add to the story's glitter. I'd go to the library and plunder all the biography and history books. Becky the Literary Pirate. Avast there, me maties!

But when I switched to contemporaries, I got lazy. I didn't think I needed to research customs and costume as much. Didn't have to get a feel for the time period because—I'm living it, right?

Wrong! You could write just what you know, but it would get repetitious after awhile. You *have* to research everything. Read up on your story's setting. Even if it's your own backyard, because—trust me—you don't know every square inch of it.

Are you really going to use all these factoid nuggets? Probably not. Too many nuggets can slow the pace of your story down to a dead stop. But a sprinkle of research gold-dust can work wonders here and there. The unwritten rule to background: Always know more than your reader about what's going on in your story.

By knowing more, you can write more. Those facts will jiggle out new ideas and offer more options for where you want your story to go. It will help you build believable landscapes and realistic characters.

So, getting back to my story, I dove head first into research—and I got unstuck. A little. The starting gate opened . . . just a crack. I could see the glimmerings of a road map ahead of me. Yes, I *could* do an outline.

I still needed to fix those opening chapters. Instead of scrapping them, I went back, scene-by-scene, and *enhanced* what had already been written, drawing on the knowledge I'd gained via research. As I reworked each scene, the gate opened wider, the words flowed easier . . . until *yes!* I knew the path from point A to point B. And even better, I could clearly see the road to all points beyond.

Now I'm not saying research holds all the keys to writer's block. But if you find yourself stuck, ask yourself: what am I missing? Chances are the answers to that question await you in the library.

Don't make my mistake. Remember, haste makes waste. You'll get farther faster if you study the racetrack before you get into the starting gate.

CHAPTER 4

Researching the Historical Romance

by Rene Miller Knudsen

S HE ADMIRES HIM ACROSS THE ROOM, thinking how handsome he looks in his velvet doublet. Or is it a cut velvet frock coat? Or maybe a buff riding jacket and nankeen breeches?

He turns to exchange a word with his good friend, Richard the Lionhearted. Or Prinny. But it could also be Billy the Kid.

Such is the dilemma for the writer of a historical romance. You have the perfect plot, a dashing hero, and a feisty heroine. But now they need a setting. How do you choose? There are all sorts of opinions, but at the end of the day, it is important to choose a setting that you feel passionate about—and can successfully research.

Along with the location, you need to choose a timeframe. Again, make it an era that you enjoy. Readers are eager to be transported for a brief time to a place far different from their reality. As a writer, you should strive to create a world vivid enough to capture your reader, sharing your attraction to this particular time and place.

For purposes of example, I'll refer to the novel I am currently working on. The story centers on a heroine who was once a great beauty, but is disfigured in a carriage accident. I had several things to consider when deciding on a setting. My heroine's injuries needed to be obvious and I didn't want her to be able to hide them. So I based my decision first by costume, nothing deeper than that. There doesn't have to be any bigger motivation for your setting.

Another factor to consider: how are the various elements of a setting going to work with your plot? In addition to costume, think about the architecture, interiors, manners, and morality of an era. Not all plots will work in every timeframe. A hero with a strong belief in the rights of man isn't going to work in a medieval setting. A heroine who firmly believes in women's suffrage won't be believable in 12th-century France. Readers want to be swept away, but not to the point of incredulity.

Now that you have your setting, you need to get comfortable with your period. When your heroine walks into a room, you should be able to describe the room she is entering with as much detail as possible. You should be able to describe her dress accurately. When she rides in a carriage, you should be able to describe what she sees. All of this *without notes*. When she talks, she should speak appropriately. Watch those anachronisms.

This isn't as difficult as it seems. If you are comfortable enough to describe detail without aids, your reader will feel it in your writing. This doesn't mean you need to be an expert on everything. If, for instance, you don't have any scenes in the kitchen, then don't worry about researching that element. Don't bother learning the costumes of domestics unless they have a significant role in your story.

How much is enough? It depends. If it's a light historical drama, then you can get away with less research. If you've chosen to write a story with heavy historical overtones, then you are going to need to dig deeper. Although my story takes place in England, I don't have a clue whom the prime minister of the time is; it's not important for the purposes of the story. But if your hero is an active member of the House of Lords, then you will need to know the history of the time. You will need to know who's who in the government and what the political controversies of the era were.

But no matter what you choose, keep in mind that it's supposed to be fun. Many writers are put off from the historical genre because of the research involved. But it doesn't have to be difficult. Yes, you will be dedicating a good chunk of time, but the rewards are well worth it.

The Internet

The Internet is incredibly convenient for an author, and a great place to begin research on nearly any topic. The wealth of material available is infinite. But as awesome as the Internet is, a word of caution. There are no standards for information disseminated. Anyone can post information whether it is accurate or not, so always double-check any information you pull from websites.

Start with the obvious. With any popular search engine, even the most basic term is bound to bring a few hits. It's wise to use more than one search engine in your work, since not all engines are the same. If you don't get any useful hits on promising sites, simplify your search terms or try another engine.

It's a good idea to bookmark sites as you visit them. You never know when you'll need to reference something again or if you'll need the information for another book. Remember to look for links at each site, as well. This is a big time-saver as you are bound to find leads to other sites you can use.

You can also search commercial sites for information. For example, if you are researching furniture for a particular time period, try looking for antique dealers. They often have a picture of items, along with a brief catalog description. Government sites are also very helpful, particularly visitor and tourism boards which are happy to provide a brief history of a town or area, often including weather, flora and fauna, and other interesting tidbits. Some give you links to maps of towns and historical sites.

Another useful trick is to use Amazon.com as a research base. You can search for a particular book, and it will show names of other books in the same category. (If some books are out of your price range, just copy down the titles and look them up in the library later.)

Author sites are another avenue. They often provide links to topical sites, so it's worth searching for a website for an author you admire or that you know writes in the same time era as your project.

But don't get lost in all of the information. It's very easy to become enmeshed in your research while losing focus of what you actually need. Keep a notebook handy. Scribble down exactly what it is you need and refer to it often. Write down any notes that are relevant or print off any pages that could prove useful, but don't spend all your available research time online.

Other Media

As great as the Internet is, books are often a better source. There is a much greater control of content, including its organization and accuracy.

There are a few books every researcher should have on their bookshelf. The first is a good dictionary—not a pocket dictionary, but a big, unabridged volume. You can find them in the cheap section at a big bookstore. I got mine at a warehouse store for less than $20. Dictionaries are wonderful sources for quick facts and terms. From a type of carriage to fabric to famous persons, a good dictionary will have a brief description. It's also useful for checking on anachronisms.

The second essential item is a historical atlas, also easily found in the discount section of a bookstore. A historical atlas is a great place to quickly see what was going on in the world during a certain time period. Considering how often the geography of the world has changed in the last several centuries, it's also an easy way to look up a country's boundaries at a certain point.

Certain areas and eras have their own historical atlases. If your focus is primarily medieval, it would be a good investment to buy an atlas dedicated to that time period. Or if you are interested in the United States, there are historical atlases specifically covering the country's history.

A good encyclopedia is also very useful. I use the one I received on CD-ROM with my computer; it does just fine for those quick facts that I need quickly. Certainly it's not a source to rely on by itself, but it's useful to answer a simple question.

Use the library as much as possible. Depending on your access to a good library, you'll need to make decisions about what you must buy and own. Costume books are very expensive, so it makes sense to borrow them if possible. If you have a college or university library nearby, investigate their policy regarding non-student lending privileges. The colleges in my community charge an annual fee for most of the same privileges as the students. Also, college libraries often have exchange programs with other libraries, so you can order books easily and get them quickly through inter-library loan programs.

A couple of tips on looking up books in the library. Many of the books I end up using, I found by browsing. Once you've found one book's call number in the catalog, go to that spot in the stacks and look around at the nearby shelves. For instance, if you are looking up historical costumes, nearby you'll find a section on celebrations. Near celebrations, there's a section on manners and customs.

When I was researching Georgian architecture, I wandered around a bit and soon saw collections of books on furniture. After finding a gem of a book on furniture, down the same row I found some great books on Georgian style. Dumb luck perhaps, but libraries do have a system of organization that encourages this, by putting related books in physical proximity.

Once you have your materials in hand, be sure to write down the call numbers of books you find most useful. Add a few notes about the book and keep these records, as a computer file or a stack of index cards, somewhere you can access them easily at a later date. Also, check the bibliographies of the best books; often they list other books from the author's sources that you can use for your own independent research.

Perhaps you find a great book with a wealth of material that doesn't apply to your current project. Make a note of it and save it for another book. But don't spend too much time on it now.

Just like doing research on the web, it's easy to get lost amongst the growing accumulation of information. Always keep a notebook handy, along with a pad of sticky notes. Keep your notes concise and close to the topic. Often you'll find yourself writing in the middle of a scene and have a quick question. It will be far less frustrating if you've kept your research handy.

I keep a large red binder with my research, including hand-written notes and pages I've printed from websites. Research for a specific novel

I keep in a file folder, along with outlines or other notes I've taken.

I find that children's books are great sources. The material is simple and easy to understand. Best part: there are lots of pictures. Check out the activity books in the children's section of your favorite local bookstore. For costumes, the paper-doll books available are infinitely useful. Others offer models of castles or ships; always rendered very colorfully and with text that's easy to read quickly.

I wouldn't recommend films or television movies as accurate research material. Too often they are wrong in many details. But they can be useful for getting a feel for a general time period. Or they might give you ideas for follow-up research. And often they shoot on location, so you can get a good visual image of an old house or countryside you are not familiar with.

Researching the historical novel is a challenging project, but full of rewards. Approach it like an adventure rather than a chore. Once you dive in, the rich world that opens before your eyes is very exciting.

And readers appreciate authors who have done their homework. Some of the most astute readers can and will spot an inaccuracy, no matter how small. So write with a view to those readers. Strive to present the best-researched novel that you can.

The hard work will pay off in the end.

CHAPTER 5

Goal Setting for the Serious Writer

by Sharon Ihle

HOW MANY OF YOU THINK that the urge to write is all you need to make it in the world of publishing? Before you decide to skip over the list of goals I've put together, please consider these facts:

1. It has been estimated that only one person in 50,000 would-be writers will sell a book.

2. Only about one person in 100 who sells a book actually makes a living at it.

For every Judith McNaught, Nora Roberts, Johanna Lindsey or Tami Hoag—in other words, those writers who travel with a secretary and a Brinks truck—there are another 100 journeymen who aren't making the mortgage payments.

Or even the payments on their computers.

With odds like that, anyone who really wants to get published in today's marketplace has to do everything he/she can to shift those odds in his/her favor. If you're driven to be that one writer in 50,000, then you may have heard that it takes determination, discipline, and lots of luck.

I can't help you with the first two requirements, but I have listed what I consider to be the eight most important steps—my idea of discipline—a writer should keep in mind to help along the way.

1. Make a long-range commitment goal.
   What do I expect to get out of my writing in the long term? How do I expect it will affect the other areas of my life? Use this goal as your overriding reason to keep writing no matter how discouraged you may get.

2. Make a list of other, smaller goals, keeping this big goal in mind.
   Think it as a family tree—smaller branches coming from a main trunk. Write these smaller goals down on 3x5 cards and keep them near your computer as a reminder. Examples: the number of pages per day you will write; time frame in which you will complete three chapters and synopsis; the days or hours you will write each week/month.

3. Make your goals realistic.
   If you struggle to produce one page of work in a given period, do *not* set your goal at 10 pages. Set it at two. Then at three. And so on.

4. Set goals to your own personality.
   Do not try to use another writer's goals or even his/her method(s) of writing. You know what works best for *you* and what makes you feel most comfortable.

5. Set a few "fantasy" goals.
   Surprisingly, these might come true as often as your core-commitment goals. Start realistically, then add to the list as each goal materializes. If you are not published, set your goal to sell a book this year. If published, set your goal to achieve the next "wish" you have on your career list.

6. Review and revise your goals.
   Your commitment goal will probably be with you awhile. The

smaller, daily goals should be reviewed often and changed where necessary. If your goal was to write three pages per day last month, and you find you can easily meet that goal . . . revise it to five pages and give yourself something new to shoot at.

7. *Never, ever* beat yourself up if you don't meet a specific goal.
   If you expect five, but only write three pages on Monday, odds are by Tuesday or Wednesday, you'll have made it up. If you consistently find yourself falling short of your goal, ease up on yourself and revise downward until you feel comfortable, but stretched.

8. Remember who's in charge.
   Only you can set your goals. Only you can take them away from yourself and remove them from your list. Don't let well-meaning friends and family do either for you.

CHAPTER 6

Top 10 Beginner's Blunders

by Shelley Bradley

1. Your manuscript doubles as artwork.

Instead, this is what editors want to see:

- *Margins*: 1" all around the page.

- *Typeface*: 10-point Courier. No proportional fonts.

- *Justification*: Left only. (A manuscript page shouldn't look like a book page.)

- *Lines per page*: 24-26. The 25-line approach is best for calculating words per page and book length.

2. Your punctuation is harder to decipher than Arabic.

You only get to make a first impression once. If you don't think enough of your work to polish it up to its grammatical best, why should an editor think enough of the book to buy it? This is easy to fix. Get help if you suspect you might need it.

It isn't the copy editor's job. Time is money. If your book is in bad shape, it may take a copy editor too long to fix to be cost-effective for the publisher to buy.

Recommended Reading: *The Elements of Style* by William Strunk Jr. and E.B. White; *The Chicago Manual of Style* by the University of Chicago Press.

3. "Was" and "were" are your favorite words.

The elusive search for verbs. Don't say "The old man walked precariously down the road." Yes, it works, but it's not as strong as possible. Instead, use "hobbled" or "limped." When writing pivotal scenes, good verbs will add extra punch.

Slay the adverb monster. You'll note that when you used the verb "walked" above, you had to add "precariously" to give the reader an image. It's easy to think of verb-adverb combinations. But the images aren't as powerful or visual. Stretch to find the verb that connotes exactly what you mean and use it mercilessly.

Use 6 words, not 11. Do you want to say, "The little house with no windows was on the rocky hill" or "The darkened cottage perched on the ridge"? Sometimes, more is less.

Recommended Reading: *Getting the Words Right* by Theodore A. Rees Cheney; *Write Tight* by William Brohaugh.

4. Discussing the weather.

Dialogue should: . . . move the plot forward or reveal character—preferably both. If it doesn't, ax it.

Identify that purpose. What is the purpose of the scene? What must you convey to the reader? Whatever it is, write all dialogue around it.

What does this say? Does each line reveal character or move the plot forward? Does it move your reader closer to the point of your scene?

Must it be said now? Do you need this line of dialogue at this point? Will the reader be able to go on and understand your story without it? If so, this information, whether conveyed in dialogue or narrative, might be best if delayed.

Recommended Reading: *Dialogue* by Lewis Turco; *Men are From Mars, Women are from Venus* by John Gray Ph.D.; *Self-Editing for Fiction Writers* by Renni Browne and Dave King; *RWA Tape* "Dialogue" (1993, Basic Track) by Julie Kistler and Tami Hoag.

5. Characters that make Dick, Jane, and Spot look complex.

History, life lessons, and dreams. Give your people a past, sprinkled with events that formed their beliefs, hopes, and fears. Give them goals. These elements give them their motivation, roundedness, and maybe allow them to become part of your epiphany—just by creating "real people."

Why the heck did he/she do that? Make sure you give each character a goal the reader can identify with—and believable reasons for wanting to achieve that goal. Without this, the reader may be asking the above question. These goals should be evident in every major scene; the dialogue and decisions of each character should point toward their individual goal.

Keep them consistent. If your hero and heroine begin the book or scene with a goal, don't have them acting contrary to it. A woman who protests against violence depicted in the media isn't likely to run out to rent *Die Hard with a Vengeance*. The best thing you can do is to really know your characters.

Recommended Reading: *Fiction is Folks* by Robert Newton Peck; *Lifetypes* by Sandra Hirsh and Jean Kummerow; *Creating Characters* by Dwight V. Swain; *Characters & Viewpoint* by Orson Scott Card.

6. What's the matter with misunderstanding and coincidence?

More than a good chit-chat. If one good conversation, without external distractions or juvenile behavior, would solve the main conflict between hero and heroine, then that conflict isn't strong enough. Why use crutches when you can run?

"She just happened to . . ." If you can finish this sentence more than once in your story to explain a plot point, then it's time to reconsider your plot. Fresh and original plots usually don't stem from or contain weak elements like coincidence.

Recommended Reading: *Techniques of the Selling Writer* by Dwight V. Swain; *Plot* by Anson Dibell; *How to Write A Damn Good Novel* by James N. Frey; *RWA Tape* "Sailing the Seven Cs."

7. Your synopsis is as easy to follow as a physics textbook.

Be a good reporter. Who, what, when, where, why, and how should be explained. The first four are relatively easy. But in reading synopses by other writers, I've noticed it's *why* and *how* that people most often neglect. If your editor doesn't understand your story, how can she love it enough to buy it?

Tell campfire stories. Your synopsis should be as entertaining as a good campfire story. Really make it work to your advantage. Make its reader not just understand the story, but *feel* at least some of the emotion you want your book's reader to feel.

Add a little sugar to the mix. Don't be afraid to put your own style into it. I once wrote part of a synopsis in one character's POV—and found it conveyed both the story's tone and that character more effectively. Even add some dialogue if you feel a scene is pivotal.

Keep it short and sweet. A caveat to the last point: don't spend so much time telling a good story in your unique style that you take 25 pages to do it. As with anything you write, examine each word and ask yourself what purpose it serves.

8. Your characters would be the best of lovers without that awful war and that pesky villain.

Conflict of Personality. What in their inherent personalities keeps them apart? Is he a cynical bachelor, while she believes in eternal love? Does he like to tell it like it is, while she avoids arguments more than my husband avoids the mall? Give them some opposite characteristics and watch the sparks fly.

Conflict of Relationship. This is the biggest stumbling block to your hero and heroine's relationship. Make it big and difficult to solve. Make them each need to grow as people before they can accept their love and future. Make it as internal as possible to really evoke the reader's emotions.

Two dogs and one bone. Also, add an external element to your plot to support the conflict of personality and relationship. This is also called conflict of circumstance. Do your hero and heroine both want to buy the same property? Want the same job? Whatever it is, let this external element lead you into, and also support, your internal conflicts. Keep in mind that a well-structured external element will bring your hero and heroine together more often.

Recommended Reading: *Conflict, Action & Suspense* by William Noble; *Scene & Structure* by Jack Bickham.

9. The first hint of conflict appears on page 100.

Dazzle them immediately. In today's TV generation, people expect to be hooked within moments. They want to be impressed right off the bat. Describing your heroine's dress or that lovely meadow across the street just isn't going to do it. Jump immediately into the conflict. Internal conflict can lead to external or vice-versa. Get your hero and heroine together and keep them together ASAP!

Backstory . . . snoozer! Don't take your first fifty pages to tell the reader what happened ten years ago. If it's relevant to the inciting event of your plot, weave it in gradually. In most cases, the reader will just need to sense that something in the past altered your hero or heroine. They don't necessarily need to see it right away. If you must begin with backstory, do it quickly and move on!

A developing friendship. Don't assume we need to know everything about your characters by page 5. Treat their entrance like an introduction to a new friend. Give the reader just enough to like them and be intrigued. Then allow the reader to really grow to know them through the course of the book.

Recommended Reading: *RWA Tape* "Pacing" by Vanessa Grant Oltmann.

10. The hero and heroine are mere backdrops to a sweeping saga.

Don't get lost. A large external plot has a tendency to occupy the spotlight in a big book. It can take root and overshadow everything if you don't carefully prune it and keep it in its place. Consider not just the external factors, but the internal ones as well, as you write each scene.

Avoid crutches. Good books require internal conflict. Leaning on large external plots to keep your hero and heroine apart is like leaning on a pair of crutches when your leg isn't broken. Make sure that what's really keeping your hero and heroine apart stems from the conflict within them (their belief structures and their aspirations), and not just from a dispute over a job or property.

Don't forget who your characters are. The easiest way to stay on track with your internal conflict is to really know who your characters are. Explore their feelings; let those become your own. Reason as they would. Ask yourself what they would do in a given situation.

Once you can answer those questions, write your scenes with that focus in mind. Always remember, romance readers read books about people and their emotions, not about things.

Section 2

Elements of Romance Storytelling

CHAPTER 7

Action

EVER FELT LIKE SCREAMING at your characters, "Don't just sit there, *do something!*" But the hero and heroine want to talk, and the villain wants to plot. Yak, yak, yak . . . yawn.

Okay, it's not the characters' fault, even though it's fun to pin the blame on them. What we need here is *action*.

As romance writers, we have it foremost in our minds that we must keep the emotional level elevated, the sexual tension tight, and the conflict constant. Thus, our stories are driven more by character than plot. We tend to internalize, since internal conflict packs more emotional punch than external. So who needs action anyway?

We do! Without action, the story just lies there. Without action, the hero never kisses the girl. Without action, the villain never gets his in the end. Without action, we'd never *see* the result of all these internally conflicted emotions!

So let's get these people moving. Your heroine must save her hero from a runaway stagecoach. This is not the time she should be recalling her fear of horses, why she was mad at the big galloot (the hero, not the horse) last Tuesday, or that she forgot to wear her riding boots. She has a man to save, and every second counts. Forget passive voice. Action needs active verbs and adjectives to get these people moving.

Here's an example of a bad action scene.

As Mary was watching the stagecoach zigzag down Main Street, she could see the sun glint off John's golden blonde hair. He sure wasn't paying attention to his driving. In fact, he looked as if he were asleep, just as he always did when she tried to tell him about the goings-on at the quilting bee. Oh, maybe he wasn't asleep! Maybe he was in trouble. Should she wake him up? He always got so mad when she interfered with his work. Like the time she tried to clean his guns and ended up shooting a hole in his Sunday boots. Boy, was he ever fit to be tied then. But look, the coach just barely missed Reverend Smith's dog, Bowser. Bowser was such a cute mutt, so friendly and good with children. Mary decided then and there she should climb on John's horse Trigger and chase the stagecoach down.

ZZZZZZZzzzzzzzzzzzzzz.

Okay, I doubt anyone ever wrote anything *that* bad! The point is: don't dally around. Get Mary off her butt and moving. Even if she's a complete airhead, she's not going to think about all those piddling details or stop to admire John's hair when lives are in danger. The deal with quilting bees, boots, and Bowser should have already been established to add the drama and conflict to the scene.

Action is living in the moment. The readers should be right there with your characters as they act and react to the given situation. Let's try the same scene again.

The stagecoach zigzagged down Main Street with John slumped over the reins. Dust rose like smoke under the horses' pounding hooves as the team careened past Mary. Reverend Smith's dog yelped as it skittered out of the way. Mary shouted for help and ran to unhitch Trigger.

Maybe the first one is funnier, but at least Mary didn't spend all day thinking about what to do this time. She reacted. There are more sensory details, too. Words like *zigzagged, slumped, pounding, careened, yelped, skittered, shouted, ran* . . . these are all active and descriptive verbs. In the first example, it's hard to tell if John is in any danger at all. In the second version, it's plain that Mary has a life-threatening situation on her hands.

So does that mean Mary shouldn't be aware of anything except the situation? No! She might realize in a flash that her heart's beating a million times a second and her knees are knocking together like cymbals. These are natural reactions.

Sometimes, it can take forever to figure out how to describe the action you see in your head. I've been brought to a complete stop struggling over one little word. One way to break through the block is to act out the scene yourself. For instance, ask your dear husband, boyfriend, or critique partner (with all due caution and care) to pretend to jump you from behind to get the feel of being attacked. Even a mild-mannered simulation will conjure up an amazing flood of sensory details and mental images.

If you don't have a theatrically inclined assistant to help you, you might try the *Romance Writer's Phrase Book* by Jean Kent and Candace Shelton. It has over 3,000 descriptive tags—some hilarious, some quite lovely—to help find the words you need to describe your action scene.

And let's not forget our dear friend, the thesaurus! I prefer using Microsoft's Bookshelf version to nail down the right shade of verb, but every writer should also keep a copy of *Roget's Thesaurus* handy.

CHAPTER 8

Location, Location, Location

IGENERALLY ADVISE: write what you know. The simplest way to choose a location is to pick a familiar area. But that can be limiting, can't it? Sometimes, it's more fun to work with a place you've never been, but for that you must do your homework.

In the case of historicals, you *must* rely on research. With futuristic stories, you have to create a brand new universe. Any way you look at it, choosing and creating your story's setting can be a daunting task.

I don't know about everybody else, but when I start a new story, I first see the characters, and then the setting. Plot comes next. I work this way because I consider the setting as one of the story's characters. The location of the story should seem as alive as our heroes and heroines. How do we take a location and turn it into a character?

If you're creating a fictional place, then toponyms can be quite helpful. A toponym is a place name that gives the reader a mini-description of the place. Names like Metropolis or Smallville give a sense of a big or small town. Or if you want your character to come from a country town, you could name it Rolling Hills or Corn Fritter.

Locale has a lot to do with how your characters act and react. People in New England differ in many ways from those of the Deep South.

Consider the local history, as well as dialects, architecture, climate, plant life, politics, current events, population density, and the physical aspects of the area. All these can help you to create realistic settings.

Here is an example of setting the stage with a colorful, image-rich sense of place from *Midnight Bayou* by Nora Roberts. She opens the novel with a perfectly creepy description:

> Death, with all its cruel beauty, lived in the bayou. Its shadows ran deep. Cloaked by them, a whisper in the marsh grass or rushes, in the tangled trap of the kudzu, meant life, or fresh death. Its breath was thick and green, and its eyes gleamed yellow in the dark.

Your setting should enhance and fit the tone of your story. A sunny day at funeral can be a mocking contrast for a character's grief . . . or rain may better suit the mood.

Whenever you are stuck looking for the proper descriptive words for setting, ask yourself—what does your character see? His or her point of view should color the way the reader perceives the scenery.

Don't get carried away, however. Pages of description on the beauty of the tropics might make wonderful prose, but it can be a real snoozer for your readers. Try to see how much you can pack in a paragraph by concentrating on three distinct details. Here's an example:

> Barley's Garage had seen better days. The painted letters on the sign out front were faded and peeling. A wooden fence stood on the far end of the gravel parking lot, its mildewed boards forming gaping holes. The rusty hood of an ancient pick-up truck was propped against it. Oddly enough, the chrome on the airplane-shaped hood ornament gleamed as if brand new.

This gives us an idea of the scene using only the sign, fence and a piece of junk. But it lacks something, since we're only given the sense of sight here and no character's point of view (POV). Think about scent, touch, taste and sound too. Let's try this paragraph again:

> The sign over Barley's Garage squeaked as it flapped in the breeze. Its faded and peeling letters read BARLY'S GARAGE to Dave's travel-weary eyes. Dust tickled his throat as he parked his car before the wooden fence in the gravel parking lot. Weeds choked the gaping holes in the mildewed boards before him. As Dave climbed from the front seat, his nose twitched at the scent of rust, machine oil and exhaust. He noticed the rusty hood of an ancient Chevy pick-up propped against the fence, squinting as the sunlight bounced off the pristine chrome of its airplane-shaped hood ornament.

Here we have more sensory details, giving the scene more character and a stronger sense of place. The reader, through the eyes of the character, has a sense of stepping into the scene.

How do you write about places you've never been? By doing as much homework as you can. Travel guides are helpful, as are atlases, almanacs, and biographies of local celebrities. Find out all you can about the history and geography of your setting.

Of course, nothing beats actually being there. If possible, arrange a "research" vacation. If not, use your friends; contact people you know who live in a particular location for their impressions. Or if you know someone who is visiting a place, ask them to pick up tourist guides and maps to hot spots, parks, and other sites of interest.

If all else fails, seek out fiction stories written by local writers. This is something you can do quite easily at most libraries by searching via geographical location under fiction categories.

For historical stories, try archaeology or art textbooks. Biographies set in that period are especially useful; they often contain information about the everyday life of the time. You also need to consider costume, weaponry, furnishings, food, modes of transportation, and customs.

For fantasy and futuristics, the sky's the limit. But remember, your brave new world must seem *real* to your readers. Be sure to create enough details, not only via geography but also by using local customs and everyday objects, to paint as vivid a picture as you can.

CHAPTER 9

Dialogue

by Patricia McLinn

YEARS OF INTERVIEWING, then editing quotes as a newspaper reporter and editor, taught me how people speak. Translating those lessons into dialogue has aided my fiction writing. Here are some of my best tips:

1. People have pet phrases.
In my book *Grady's Wedding*, I borrowed a southern friend's favorite multi-purpose expression to give to the southern heroine, Leslie Craig: "Bless your heart."

A little girl's "Can I ask you somethin'?" in my novel *Wedding of the Century* starts as an innocuous question, but builds through the book to reveal important information.

In *Not a Family Man*, the hero Tucker Gates thinks of the heroine's ex-husband as "a piece of work." If Jenny (the heroine) then also thought of her ex-husband in the same terms, it would jar attentive readers and undermine Tucker's voice. The only exception is if another character uses that phrase *deliberately*, to make a clear, specific point. In this case, the reader must recognize it as intentional.

For example, if Tucker referred to Jenny's ex-husband as "a piece of work" in speaking to Jenny, and she then used it later, it could signal a change in her attitude toward the breakup of her marriage. Note: the character who "owns" the phrase has to have said it out loud—otherwise you're setting up your phrase-borrower as a mind reader.

Tip: *Let your characters have "personal belongings" in their speech that stay personal.*

2. People use a lot of words to say very little.
In journalism, that's the primary reason for the development of ellipses—to indicate hunks taken out by a reporter or editor that could most easily be paraphrased as blah, blah, blah. If you want to make anyone appear boring, stupid, or pompous, quote them verbatim. The same goes for fiction. But as fiction writers, we get to skip the ellipses and allow our characters to get to the point.

Tip: *Rescue your characters from overspeaking.*

3. People rely on favorite qualifiers.
Examples of common qualifiers: *generally, usually, normally, most times, perhaps, maybe, almost, nearly, just about, pretty near.*

These are words people use automatically. (Words used without conscious thought reveal inner character, so they are powerful tools for building a character's voice.) Most people would not use the full spectrum of qualifiers. Typically, an individual settles into using one or two and remains loyal to them.

The same character, though, might use different qualifiers to indicate his/her mood. But try to differentiate from one character to another. For instance, one character could use "generally" (in formal speech) and "usually" (in casual speech). Another might use "as a rule" (formal) and "normally" (casual).

Tip: *Give your characters individuality.*

4. People speak in abbreviated form.
They rarely start at the beginning and go to the end. And in real life, they never say everything that you, as the writer, would like them to cover.

In journalism, I knew a reporter who would have quotes like: "We're really going to do great against the Mets in Sunday's game, which starts at 1 p.m. at Wrigley Field, with an expected sellout crowd," said Sammy Sosa.

Did Sammy really say all that? I doubt it.

Tip: *Don't make your characters' dialogue carry all the weight of complete information.*

5. People generally do not say what their listeners already know.

Listen to this:

> As my best friend, Drucilla, you know that I am the third daughter of the Count of Cranberries. And I hate the restrictions and requirements that position puts on me.

You have to wonder about the speaker's taste in best friends if her old companion Drucilla can't keep these facts about her in mind. (Note: If your intention is to create an annoying character, this is one way to do it.)

So, how do you get information across when the characters know it, but the reader doesn't? Here's one way:

> "I don't know why I can't run barefoot through the fields like you and the peasant girls do, Drucilla."
>
> "Because you are not a peasant girl. I love you as a sister, but as the daughter of a count—"
>
> "Third daughter. And of the Count of Cranberries, for heaven's sake."
>
> "Nevertheless, you have certain responsibilities and—"
>
> "An image to uphold," Prudence picked up the refrain wearily.

Tip: *Do not let your characters make speeches. Let them talk.*

6. What is said looks very different when written down.

In a newspaper article, I once quoted a woman whose son was training as an Olympic diver. She later claimed I misquoted her. I played her the tape. "But I didn't mean it that way!" she said.

Your characters might not mean it the way it's written, either. Read dialogue out loud. Try emphasizing different words to see if that changes the meaning—because readers will place their own emphasis where they choose.

Punctuation can direct the emphasis. Italics can add emphasis. However, overuse of italics makes characters sound as if they are overreacting. Also, overuse of this technique can make the italics lose their punch.

Instead of italics, try rewriting so the right words say exactly what your character means, rather than gambling your reader will hit on that meaning. This is a major advantage of writing dialogue—you have the power and the time to find the right words.

Tip: *Don't let your characters' words look different from the meaning you intended.*

7. Readers give more weight to what someone says in dialogue than to all the rest of it.

I had a newspaper editor who said: "It doesn't matter if you know it—get someone to say it."

In fiction, this is especially important. Dialogue is the most direct communication between character and reader, and therefore the most powerful.

That's also why it's so important to keep the character's dialogue consistent and believable. Any lapse will remind the reader of you, the writer. It's better to avoid that authorial intrusion, because to the reader, their direct communication with the character is personal.

A corollary: studies show that readers scan newspaper stories for quotes. Anecdotal information and logic suggest the same is true for dialogue in fiction.

Tip: *What your character says has more impact on the reader than what you tell.*

8. People repeat for emphasis and when they are feeling strong emotion.

Often, this occurs in three's. When the Count of Cranberries finds out about his daughter's behavior, he is likely to say:

> "I will not have you going barefoot. I will not have you running through the fields. I will not have you acting like a peasant girl."

Also, note his lack of contractions. The Count of C says: "I will not" rather than "I won't." That formality adds emphasis.

Two famous presidential denials could have started "I'm not a . . ." and "I didn't have . . ." Instead, they chose "I am not a . . ." and "I did not have . . ." for emphasis.

Contractions, or lack of them, contribute to characterization in all dialogue. In my novel, *Hidden in a Heartbeat*, the heroine's controlling grandmother never uses contractions. That's an extreme, as befitted an extreme character. Most people of all ages and station will use "I'm," "you're," "it's," "don't" and other standard contractions. Having a character use "I'd've," on the other hand, says something about the character and the circumstances (likely informal, possibly aiming for levity.)

Tip: *Repetition and contractions convey your characters' emotions.*

9. People talk in rhythms that are as individual as facial expressions.

These rhythms tell a great deal about the person. They can indicate age, gender, place of origin, ethnicity, education, occupation, and relationship to those around them. Components of rhythm include:

- Contractions (or lack of them).

- Placement of modifiers.

- Introductory phrases (or the lack of them) such as I think, perhaps if we, etc.

- Dropping pronouns. "Going to the store" instead of "I'm going to the store."

- Using "that" in dialogue. "I said that I would be on a panel" vs. "I said I'd be on a panel."

- Length of words, sentences, paragraphs.

The last element I mentioned, length, also indicates emotion. When people are excited, angry, happy or experiencing any strong emotion, their talk tends to be short and choppy. People tend to speak in longer, convoluted rhythms when they're trying to impress or fool someone—including themselves.

Tip: *Rhythm gives your characters a signature sound.*

I haven't covered all of the elements of rhythm, but you can discover them yourself by following the last rule I learned from interviewing:

10. Listen.
In interviewing, it's obvious you have to listen. But how can this help you write fiction?

- Eavesdrop. Restaurants, malls, trains, and sidewalks are prime opportunities.

- Tune into talk radio; undistracted by body language, you're listening to pure dialogue.

- Tape a family dinner, then listen for the individual rhythms and idiosyncrasies, as well as family traits.

- Watch movies with particular attention to how character is built through speech.

Tip: *To help your characters talk well, listen carefully.*

CHAPTER 10

Imagery
The "3-Item" Method

THE WORD "IMAGERY" ITSELF suggests a lyrical picture, doesn't it? Look it up in a thesaurus, and you'll get these synonyms: *images, descriptions, metaphors, similes*. These related terms suggest some techniques we use to paint our imagery.

However, some of us have a hard time painting a vivid picture. Perhaps we can "see" the image we want to convey to the reader in our mind's eye, but when we try to put those images down on paper, the clear focus fades away.

So how do we paint a picture with words?

The 3-Item Method

I use this method all the time. You simply take three items present in a setting and describe them. The beauty of this approach is it allows you to describe just enough for the reader to get a sense of the scene, without letting the prose get in the way of the story's action.

Brevity is one of its greatest appeals. Personally, I've stopped reading a book after an author took too many pages to describe a landscape.

Why? Because although getting a feel for the lay of the land was nice, by the second paragraph, I already got the point. No further description was needed. By the second page, I was bored. By the time the author returned to the story's action, I had to thumb back to find out where she'd left off.

Never fall in love with the incredibly detailed pictures you *can* paint with words. Paint the picture in a simple but effective form, then get the heck out of there.

A first exercise

The 3-item method will help you paint that picture. Let's say you want to describe a room. Let's make it a bedroom. First, pick out three items in the room to describe.

Wallpaper, Bed, End-table.

Okay, we have our three items. Now, we'll describe them.

> Red-and-white striped wallpaper coated Clara's bedroom walls like an enormous candy cane. The canopy bed had a white iron frame with an intricate heart-shaped headboard. White iron leaves wound around the bedposts, spearing into the muted red canopy at the top and disappearing into the matching chenille spread at the bottom. A collection of glass cats crouched and prowled across the white enamel surface of the neighboring end table, surrounding the gilt-framed picture of Clara's father.

Sort of gives you the impression of a child's room, doesn't it? Or if Clara is a grown woman, maybe she's a bit childish emotionally. Or maybe she's lonely. All she has to keep her company is her glass cats and a picture of her father.

When using imagery to describe a scene, it is also an opportunity for characterization. The room in which a person lives in says a lot about their personality, so I purposely used descriptive words that I thought would characterize Clara. Use this technique to your advantage.

As you can see, by simply picking out three items in the room, I can give you a sense of how it looks and feels—in one paragraph. I didn't have to stop the story for a whole page (or more) while I described every little detail.

Notice I used active rather than passive voice. A sure way to turn any passage into a snoozer is to use passive voice. Stick to active verbs instead. Also, whenever possible, use adjectives instead of adverbs. Adjectives pack more muscle to keep your prose rolling along. Also take note that I used our old friend, the simile, in the phrase "like an enormous candy cane."

Add a Point of View

But something is missing. Can you guess what it is?

If you said point of view, you're right. The sample paragraph has a detached feel to it because there is no point of view. It's simply a dry description, with no emotion or personal reaction to the surroundings. So let's try it again, this time adding another character's point of view.

> Carl hated visiting Clara's room. It always felt as if he'd stepped back in time. She hadn't moved so much as a pillow in ten years. Red-and-white striped wallpaper coated her bedroom walls like a candy cane. The canopy bed had a white iron frame with an intricate heart-shaped headboard.
>
> White iron leaves wound around the bedposts, spearing into the muted red canopy at the top and disappearing into the matching chenille spread at the bottom. A collection of glass cats crouched and prowled across the white enamel surface of the neighboring end table, surrounding the gilt-framed picture of their father.
>
> Their father. Carl couldn't understand why Clara insisted on keeping a picture of the man who'd abandoned them ten years ago at her bedside. If he had his way, he'd rip it to shreds instead.

As you can see, I really didn't change that much. But by adding in Carl's reaction to his surroundings, I'm able to toss in a bit of backstory and characterization. I not only describe the scene, but also tell you something about the people living in it.

Doing this will make the difference between a vivid and faded picture. To paint a vivid picture, you must put life in it.

Get the picture

Still having problems describing what you see in your mind's eye? Many authors like to work with a *real* picture sitting on the desk beside them. This is often very helpful to me, but a word of caution. Don't use who or what is in the picture as the whole of your description. You want to use that as a starting point only; then reach beyond into the details of your imagination and the particulars of your story.

Another common device (overused in my opinion, although I'm guilty of using it) is to use a simile of a well-known person or place.

> He looked like a taller version of Tom Cruise.

> The green hills reminded her of a scene from THE QUIET MAN.

Try to avoid this kind of easy description, which often proves dated or limited in audience. Yes, it's a convenient short-cut. But go to the well too many times, and you'll find that your story will start sounding like you got your descriptions out of a magazine.

Strive for originality, and your writing will grow stronger.

Pull readers in

Here's another example of the 3-item approach, this one from Linda Howard's novel, *Mr. Perfect*.

> The late afternoon spun away. From somewhere up the street she heard a child shriek with laughter. A car drove by. The faint sound of hedge clippers drifted to her ears.

With three simple items, Linda describes the sights and sounds of a neighborhood street. If you can teach yourself to keep your descriptions focused, appealing to a range of senses and playing off simple but clear images that your readers can relate to, you'll succeed in drawing your readers into the story.

Once readers are *inside* the scene, their imaginations can begin to fill in the rest of the details. And when imaginations are in play, you've got them hooked.

Sometimes the simplest techniques are the most effective.

CHAPTER 11

How to Handle Internal Monologues

ONE SURE WAY to get readers involved in your characters is to show them the inside of their heads. No, I'm not talking about brain surgery. I'm talking about internal monologues— showing what your characters are thinking. By revealing your characters' thoughts, you give them depth. And these silent monologues give readers a better understanding of the characters' motivations and, more importantly, their internal conflicts.

So let's *think* about this! How much thinking should your characters do? You don't want internal monologues to run on for pages and pages. This slows the pacing of your story to a crawl. Instead, sprinkle in your characters' thoughts here and there, wherever needed, but let the action and dialogue of your story carry the reader along.

How to show thoughts

How do you show what your characters are thinking? Some authors employ italics, but beware of overuse. Use italics only to emphasize key thoughts. For example, the moment when your hero comes to the realization he can't live without your heroine (or vice versa).

The important criteria is that, as your readers step inside a character's head, the transition should feel seamless to the reader. You can ease the way by simply using an attributive tag, such as:

> Wow, Jack thought. Mary still has great legs.

Or maybe you want to try something more subtle, like:

> Jack's gaze skimmed down to Mary's ankles. Wow! She still has great legs.

Either way, we know we're now inside Jack's head and that he admires Mary's legs. In the second case, you are cueing the reader in by showing the character in action, followed by his thought. So you don't always need to include an attributive phrase with each thought. If it's clear who is doing the thinking, let those thoughts flow!

Thoughts and backstory

Often, writers use flashbacks to show a character's backstory. This can be a tricky technique. A common beginner's mistake is to start their book by immediately taking the reader into the past. One moment the reader is in the present; the next, they realize they have spent the last ten pages experiencing something that happened in the past. By the time you bring them back, the readers don't remember *when* you started!

Instead, allow backstory to trickle out over the course of the book. Characters can reveal their past via dialogue and also through snippets of internal monologue. If you feel you *must* use a flashback, keep it as short as possible.

My suggestion: begin and end the flashback portion of the scene in past perfect tense. But let the rest of the action and dialogue within the flashback proceed in simple past tense, instead of a long internal monologue. For example:

> It had been over fifteen years since Mary had last tangled with Jack Rite. He had sneered at her as he'd told her goodbye.

> "You'll never be good enough for me, Mary. I need a woman who
> can stand on her own, not a clinging vine like you."
> "But Jack, I thought you loved me!"
> "I never said I loved you. And I never will."
> She had cried for days . . . and even now it hurt to remember.

Poor Mary. Don't worry; I'm sure she'll make him eat those words—since he's so fond of her legs and all. The main point is to make sure you let the readers know *when* they are at all times. Clearly, a short flashback that *shows* what Jack did can be more effective than pages of Mary telling the reader how he hurt her.

Thoughts within dialogue

Using thought within dialogue can be an effective way to show conflict. Just don't let those thoughts take over the characters' conversations.

Here's an example:

> "Mary, would you mind taking this report upstairs to Mr. Rite?"
> Mary thought she'd rather chew on glass than see Jack Rite again.
> "Of course not, Ms. Reed," she said. "It'd be my pleasure."

See how easy that is? It's clear Mary doesn't want to see Jack, although she doesn't let her feelings show to Ms. Reed. The readers quickly see those conflicted feelings with a quick peek inside Mary's head.

A peek is usually all you need. There are other times when the character might have deeper issues to ponder. The key thing is knowing when enough is enough. Remember, internal monologue can slow the pace of a story. But sometimes you need a pause to let your readers catch their breath.

Now and then, spending some time with a character's thoughts can be an excellent technique to involve readers with your characters in a deeper way. Just don't make it seem like a permanent vacation from your story.

CHAPTER 12

The Rules of Point of View

POINT OF VIEW . . . it's a never-ending debate for writers and a favorite topic for workshops at conferences. Often, new writers don't understand exactly what "point of view" (POV) means, what the "rules" are, and when the rules can be broken. They get critiques with notes like, "POV! You can't have the hero thinking this," but without an explanation of why.

As a starting point, conventional wisdom says the following:

- A writer should stick to one POV per scene. "Head-hopping" (switching back and forth in a single scene between two characters' perspectives) is a definite no-no.

- For category romance, a book should either contain just the heroine's POV, or optionally the heroine's and hero's POVs.

- Multiple POVs should be reserved for single-title works only.

- In general, third-person POV is the preferred viewpoint.

Now you might be saying, "But what about Nora Roberts? Or Judith

McNaught? They head-hop all the time. And look at Diane Gabalon—she used first person in her Outlander series!"

These common objections are frequently heard whenever someone speaks on this subject. The speaker's reply is also predictable: "Well, when you sell as many books as they have, then you can head-hop too."

It's a fair answer, I guess, and most likely a correct one. But for a beginning writer, that answer doesn't satisfy.

So let's first look more closely at what POV is, then we'll get down to reviewing the rules and considering their validity.

Whose Point of View?

Consider this example:

> Brad scrubbed his devastatingly handsome face, combed his rich russet hair, then pulled a T-shirt over his rippling, corded muscles.

What's wrong with this sentence? Well, if this story is being told from Brad's POV, and unless he has an ego the size of Canada, he would not describe his own appearance this way. It is an example of author intrusion. Brad's POV would probably go more like this:

> Brad scrubbed his face, combed his hair, then pulled on a T-shirt.

Or if you want Brad to consciously describe himself, maybe it could go like this:

> Brad looked in the mirror and thought, not bad. His face wouldn't scare small children. His reddish-brown hair had been recently trimmed and the hours he'd spent in the weight room seemed to be paying off on his biceps.

He hardly seems a hero to write home to mum about, does he? But realize, Brad is looking at himself through his own eyes. Unless he's utterly vain, he's not going to describe himself in glowing terms.

So, if you want readers to drool over the man, you need to describe him from someone else's POV:

> Cece watched Brad scrub his devastatingly handsome face, comb his rich russet hair, then pull a T-shirt over his rippling, corded muscles.

Does that seem like we're back where we started? Not quite. The key difference is that in this last example, we're seeing Brad from Cece's POV, not Brad's or the author's.

That's what POV is all about: getting inside a character's head, seeing through her eyes what she sees, thinking what she thinks, and feeling what she feels.

Common errors

The most common POV error is when a writer accidentally steps out of the POV he/she is using to describe a character's physical reactions. For instance, if a man were creeping up behind Cece, she wouldn't be able to see him do that—since in her POV, he's behind her. Maybe she could hear or smell him, but not see him. She also couldn't see her own expression of surprise. Once she realized it, she'd certainly feel her pulse pound, her eyes go wide, and her mouth drop open in shock. But she couldn't see him behind her, and logically could not see her own face and its expressions.

The same applies to emotional and internal reactions. A character (unless psychic) cannot get inside another character's head. Brad can *guess* Cece wants him, but he can't *know* it, unless she says or does something to prove it. This is probably good for Cece, and it's definitely good for you. Why? Because by using POV correctly, you can keep the characters guessing about each other's feelings. This is a terrific tool you can use to increase tension and conflict.

If you decide it will help your story to get inside a person's head and use his/her POV, remember to be consistent and logical. Keep in mind the limitations of what that person can actually sense, and you'll be okay

Reconsidering the Rules

Let's get back to those conventional-wisdom rules of POV, starting with the last one:

- *Third person is the preferred point of view.*

First, what is third person?

Third person is telling a story from an objective standpoint, sort of like a report from a bystander. "He was . . . She was . . . " and so on.

In such cases, the author narrates the story (but not from the perspective of someone who is actually in the story). The author is using the "third person" or third-party voice. Most popular fiction is written from this perspective. But is this the best way to tell *your* story?

Another choice is to use first person. A first-person story is one told from a subjective viewpoint. "I was . . . The next thing I knew . . ." and so on.

In such cases, the main character narrates the story (that is, you, as author, write as if you were the main character narrating the story as it happens to him or her.)

When done well, first-person POV provides an intimate relationship between the reader and the character. Diane Gabaldon's *Outlander* is an excellent example.

For me, some of the best first person writing is the Dave Robicheaux series by James Lee Burke. I recommend *The Neon Rain* and *Heaven's Prisoners* as fine examples of how wonderful this POV can be.

Second person? This is more difficult and hasn't been used often in a novel-length work. This is the "you" POV. If you're interested in reading a story that was told in this way, try *Bright Lights, Big City* by Jay McInerney.

So yes, there have been successful authors who have broken the "Third person is the preferred POV" rule. In general, though, most editors will turn down or be more critical of stories told in first or second. But if you feel your story requires it, there is good precedent to back up your belief.

Category or single-title?

The next rule is:

- *Category romance prefers either one POV, or both the hero's and heroine's.*

The second option—using both the hero's and heroine's viewpoints—means alternating back and forth between them in some fashion.

In general, this rule is also true for the most part. I've heard category editors say they will "consider" multiple POVs. But the reality is this: category novels are usually shorter than single-title ones. So in practice, you'll find it hard to meet your word-count limits if you take the time in a category novel to explore the POVs of secondary characters.

If category romance prefers just one, or at the most two POVs, does this mean the opposite: that you must use many multiple POVs if you writing single-title works? No, it doesn't. But again, there's a practical side to this. If you are writing a longer single-title work, you'll have to come up with innovative ways to keep your plot moving along. And with important subplots, it will be more difficult to support them without those secondary characters and their independent perspectives and views.

Remember James Lee Burke? Well, as his Dave Robicheaux series grew, he experienced problems in sticking with first-person voice. He managed to work around it by having secondary characters relate events Dave didn't know about directly, using a variety of "as told to me" techniques. It was well done, but it demonstrates how difficult it is to sustain complex stories using only one POV.

"Head-hopping"

This brings us at last to one of the most hotly debated "rules" of POV.

- *A writer should stick to one POV per scene.*

Head-hopping—shall it be permitted or not? Now, let's all play nice and not get in a tizzy over this. Head-hopping is the technique of switching back and forth between POVs throughout a single scene. The danger: If you aren't a Nora Roberts or a Judith McNaught, this approach can make your readers dizzy and confused.

And lord help you if your reader is a writer, because I've known some (okay, including me) who will throw a book across the room if the POV changes five times in a single paragraph.

Unless done skillfully by a masterful writer, it can be frustrating to read. Who's thinking what? This is why beginning authors are advised to stick with one POV per scene. Think of it as a consideration for your manuscript's safety.

What does Nora and Judith know that we don't know? *Transitions.* These ladies are very, very, good at making smooth changes from one character's POV to the next.

Here's brief example of head-hopping, using the lovelorn Cece and Brad:

> Cece was sick of watching Brad comb his rich russet hair.
> Brad wished Cece would quit staring at him.

As you can see, the first sentence is in Cece's POV; it tells us how she feels. Then comes the second sentence—in this case, a new paragraph in the same scene—and we're in Brad's head now. The POV switch is clear, because I signaled it with the phrase: "Brad wished."

It's as simple as that to change POV successfully, but you must make it clear which character is "speaking." But I strongly recommend that you limit your POV switches. Changing within the paragraph, or even the same sentence, is *very* confusing.

If you must head-hop, at least keep the POV switches separated from paragraph to paragraph to help clarify the transitions.

Exceptions

From a personal standpoint, I try to stay in one POV per scene . . . most of the time. The one justifiable exception is a love scene. A love scene without *both* points of view, I believe, packs less emotional punch. If I am writing a love scene, I do tend to shift back and forth between the characters, from paragraph to paragraph.

In a few other cases, for specific plot purposes, I might feel the need to shift the tension from one character to another by switching POVs. But if I do make such a shift within a scene, I try to do it only once.

The writer's friend

Remember, staying with one POV serves a writerly purpose. It can increase tension and conflict because of the element of mystery. If a character doesn't know exactly what another character is thinking, it can lead to interesting speculations, misconceptions, and later surprises.

POV is a writer's best friend in other ways, too. Let's say you have a scene that's just not working. Try rewriting it from another character's POV. Sometimes, by shifting your own perspective to see it through the eyes of a different character, you will discover new aspects to a scene, and it will unfold more easily.

Here's a last tip: to check for potential POV problems, ask a critique partner or someone you trust to go through your scenes and mark each time the POV shifts. (It's hard for writers to see their own work with as objective an eye.)

Then look at the shifts and ask yourself if they're necessary or even intended. *You* know whose POV you're in, but do your readers?

There you have it, a closer look at the "rules" of POV. Do they apply to your story? Ask any writer you meet and they'll have an opinion. But only you can answer that. Weigh the practical considerations of what sells against the artistic considerations of what you think works for your story and your writing style.

If you ask me, no *rule* of writing is absolute. Variety is what gives us our own voice and distinct style. Listen to the voice inside. More often than not, it'll steer you to the right answer.

CHAPTER 13

Love Scenes

I HAVE AN UNFRIGID (she made me say this) friend who *hates* to write love scenes. No, she *abhors* writing love scenes. It's not that she's inhibited; she just feels she cannot connect with the words being written.

Now me . . . I *enjoy* writing love scenes! There, I've said it, and I'm not red in the face about it at all.

Am I a sex maniac? Certainly not! I look at love scenes as the ultimate challenge a romance writer (or any writer for that matter) can face. Your mission is to take the simple act of love between a man and woman, an act as old as time, and make it fresh and new. You want your reader's pulse to pound; you want them to feel what your lovers feel.

Sound tough? Not really. The key thing to remember is that this is *your* story. There are no rules . . . well, only the ones that exist within your mind.

First off, let's get one thing straight. I'm talking about love scenes, not sex scenes. A sex scene is about mechanics, not emotion. I'm talking about love scenes which, if you'll pardon the unintentional pun, are the climax of the sexual tension and attraction your hero and heroine feel for each other. How far they go depends on how far *you* want to go.

A wonderful thing about the romance genre is there's room for all kinds of love stories, from the sweet to the steamy. So if you want to leave it to the reader's imagination what goes on behind the bedroom door, feel free to do so.

Where to start?

First, ask yourself what you want to accomplish with this scene. Are your characters taking their relationship to the next level? Will making love bring them closer or drive them apart?

The emotional conflicts involved should be clear before the first kiss. These conflicts can be anything: inhibitions, class differences, trust vs. control issues, and so on. The point is that your love scene should have a purpose to advance your plot. Neither character should walk away without feeling changed in some way.

So first try to understand *why* you want to write this scene. What should it accomplish?

Next consider why your characters chose *this point in the story* to make love? And review why they chose this person as a lover. Are they thinking with their hearts or with their heads (or with some lopsided combination thereof)?

Here's my opinion: your characters may be from opposite ends of the spectrum, but there's got to be some common ground, some identifying factor that brings them together before they make love. Without that, you have a sex scene, not a love scene.

Keep in mind that we all have inner issues and preconceived notions about sex. Those conflicts and considerations should be part of your characters' attitudes too. There has to be something between your lovers besides pheromones. By showing what that bond is, your love scene will have depth and emotional punch.

Emotions and sensations

You've decided that for the purposes of your plot, your story needs a love scene. But you still feel uncomfortable writing it. Maybe it's a case of writerly inhibitions. Or maybe you're just worried that your scene will fall victim to the dreaded purple prose. (Frankly, I like a tinge of violet in my love scenes . . . but that's just me.)

Or maybe describing action isn't your forte. Whatever the case, relax. You *can* do this!

Let's talk about that dreaded violet tint for a moment. Our genre gets criticized all the time for being the home of purple prose. I guess it's okay for "literary" works to ramble on and on—oh, forget it. The important question to ask ourselves is what do *we* like to read?

That's what matters to good storytelling—and to commercial success as well. Always think of the reader, and put yourself in that person's place. Your own sensibilities are as a good place to start as any. Do you just want a detailed description of the physical actions? Or do you want emotions involved, too?

The clear answer for romance fiction is: yes, we want emotions, too. But how do we describe our characters' feelings? Emotions are intangible. But in a love scene, they are also wrapped up in the senses—sight, smell, taste, sound, and touch.

What do the physical sensations feel like? And what do the lovers feel *internally*? Those are two *very* different questions, and in romance, they both should be answered.

To describe emotion and sensation in romance, writers often use metaphors and similes to avoid sounding clinical. At the same time, the best writers also employ active verbs and adjectives to show the urgency of the action underway.

Here are a few quick examples:

> What choice did she have? His fingers stroked her to flash point, and everything happened at once. Her body tightened like a fist. Lights whirled in front of her eyes, spinning to the roar of sound in her head that was her own frantic heartbeat.
>
> —from MONTANA SKY, by Nora Roberts

Note the simile, "tightened like a fist," and the active verbs and adjectives, "flash, stroked, whirled, spinning, roar, frantic."

> Anticipation wound like a spring inside her, tighter and tighter, pounding for release . . . until the anticipation exploded into a firestorm of sensation.
>
> —from NIGHT SINS, by Tami Hoag

The ellipses in the passage are mine; my apologies for skipping a few sentences. But note the simile, "like a spring." See the active words, "tighter, pounding, exploded," and the metaphors, "pounding for release" and "firestorm of sensation."

> Christina couldn't speak, couldn't think. Lyon was pulling her into the sun. Soon, when she could bear the scorching heat no longer, he would give her sweet release.
>
> —from THE LION'S LADY, by Julie Garwood

Here we have the metaphor, "pulling her into the sun," and the adjectives "scorching" and "sweet."

> She sank her nails into Nick's skin and took fierce pleasure in the shudder that went through him. A glorious sensation of wild heady freedom flowed in her veins. She abandoned herself to her own womanly power.
>
> —from ZINNIA, by Jayne Castle (Jayne Ann Krentz)

The metaphor here is "wild heady freedom flowed in her veins." Active verbs and adjectives, "fierce, shudder, abandoned."

The first two examples are from contemporary stories. The third comes from a historical, and the fourth is from a futuristic novel.

Contemporary stories tend to employ action over metaphor. It's often the opposite for historicals, probably because they use a more lyrical prose style overall. Speaking of historicals, traditional Regencies seem to stop at the bedroom door, although there are, of course, exceptions.

In a survey taken on the Romance Central website, the majority of participants said they prefer "steamy" love scenes. It's notable that many writers use metaphors of heat and fire when creating love scenes. Well, passion is supposed to be hot, isn't it?

But in writing love scenes, steamy or otherwise, aren't you often in danger of setting yourself up to sound repetitious?

Not necessarily. The answer is to realize that great love scenes should be character-driven. If proper attention is given to characterization in the scene, then that will make it as original as your characters.

Avoiding common problems

A few years ago, I attended a workshop on love scenes by author Glenda Saunders. In it, she mentioned that before she sits down to write such a scene, she takes out her thesaurus and writes down a list of descriptive words to fit that scene.

I take a similar approach. I choose a "theme" of sorts for the scene—perhaps something involving water, or music, or poetry—and work within that for the metaphors and similes I choose.

But how to avoid the dreaded purple prosies? Certainly there is a danger of overusing metaphors and similes.

A useful tip: read your scenes out loud. Yes, I said *out loud!* If you're shy about this, then wait until you have a moment alone.

Why? Because this technique is a great way to eradicate purple-prose overload. If the draft of the scene sounds silly to your ears, chances are it will sound silly to everyone else, too.

Better yet, find someone you trust to critique the scene for you. I know for new writers this can be painful, especially for an intimate scene. But objective feedback is worth its weight in gold.

The key thing to remember is that less is more. People want to know what's going through the characters' hearts and heads during the scene. Similes and metaphors can help you achieve that, but only to a point. What grabs the reader and puts them in the scene are the *active verbs* and *adjectives*. They're precise, they're descriptive, and they express thoughts and feelings in the way most people actually think.

To keep the readers in the moment, use active verbs over passive. This will make you eliminate the "he was . . . she was . . ." sentences from your scene. Remember: active verbs put you in the moment; passive verbs distance you from it.

Slang and euphemisms

Let's be honest, have you ever thought of the male genitalia as a "fleshy blade"? No, I didn't think so, but I bet if we took a show of hands of readers who've read this in a historical love scene, all arms would be up!

Or here's one of my all-time favorites from the contemporary hit parade: "throbbing love muscle"! *Ewww!*

Still, romance readers don't want clinical descriptions for body parts either. Slang words can make your scene more realistic, but overuse can reduce it to the level of porn.

You need description and action, but also weigh how graphic it should be. Consider how it will lessen or enhance the emotional impact of the scene. If you review the examples of good writing given on the previous pages, you can see how top-flight writers blend descriptive words with metaphors to achieve a balance.

Last Tips

A brief word on point of view: If you're going to head-hop (see previous chapter), then love scenes are the only time it should be allowed, in my opinion. A recent Romance Central website survey did confirm that readers prefer multiple POVs in love scenes—probably because that's the best way to show how the hero and heroine act and react to each other.

Still, in some cases you may choose to stay in a single POV if you wish to keep the other person's reactions a mystery.

Clearly, the choice is up to you. Weigh the emotional impact this scene has on your story. Review its purpose—what the scene will achieve for your story—and write accordingly.

That's what a love scene is supposed to do—provide emotional impact. In my opinion, the presence of too many love scenes in a story diminishes their impact. Once you take your characters beyond the bedroom door, I don't think you need to keep repeating it.

Unless, of course, the next love scene offers a new or different perspective to the growth of their relationship.

When in doubt, let your characters be your guide. Trust me, they are often the best advisers to listen to. In writing love scenes, listen carefully to their desires and demands, to their hopes and dreams, and yes, to their fears and foibles.

And then write that scene that will move your story forward—and satisfy your readers' genuine interest in both the physical act of love and all the powerful emotions that go with it.

CHAPTER 14

Plotting
Your Way

by Shelley Bradley

PEOPLE FREQUENTLY TELL ME they want to write a book, but don't know where to start. Every writer you know, even your favorites, all went through this same dilemma. Personally, I've been writing now for nearly ten years. Along the way, I've picked up a number of plotting techniques that claim to help writers get started. Some worked for me. Some didn't.

I was not always certain why I preferred one method over another. But after writing several books and critiquing with friends who were writing their own works, I came to a stunning conclusion: the differences in how writers respond to varied plotting methods reflects the fact that everyone views the world just a bit differently.

Of course they do, you say. Yes, but it becomes a fundamental issue when you're trying to plot a book. Based on who you are and how you see the world, you are generally one of two kinds of plotter:

1. *Plot-driven*. If you've begun piecing a story together in your head or on notecards, you may notice that your plot revolves around a series

of external events to which your character(s) react. Most action-adventure plots fall into this category.

Typically, these books open with a blast, finish with a bang, and are heavy on pacing and action.

2. *Character-driven.* If the story spinning in your mind is more about people—what drives them, what makes them feel, change, want, hate, and love—you are probably writing a character-driven book.

Most Jane Austen books fall into this category, for instance. You see no bombs exploding in Elizabeth Bennet's world in *Pride and Prejudice*, do you? No, you see her and Mr. Darcy and their attempts to understand one another and become better people.

Have you decided what type of plot most appeals to you? If so, good. If not, you might be protesting that you like both kinds of plots. So do I. I own a copy of *Speed* and I've probably watched Keanu Reeves play the role of Jack about twenty times. But I also love *Dangerous Liaisons* and consider watching the intrigues of Glenn Close, Michelle Pfeiffer, and John Malkovich a wonderful treat. They're two totally different movies, right? Yes, and if you like both types, that can help you balance your plots to appeal to both audiences.

But alas, most of us gravitate to one plot type or another. As long as you know your preferences—your natural biases when you're plotting—you'll be sure not to plan too many explosions or deceptions in your story.

Once you know which type of plot you're most inclined to write, how does that help you come up with a plot that makes sense?

A few years ago, I discovered the plotting method that screenwriters use, which seems to benefit both plot-driven and character-driven writers. For more detail about this approach, read *Screenplay* by Syd Field, available in bookstores everywhere.

Here's a simple summary of that plotting strategy.

The inciting event

First, you begin the book with an inciting event, the happening that begins your entire story. Don't begin by telling the reader all about your character. We don't care about someone we don't know yet. We want to see them in action, to see their dilemma portrayed before us.

In the movie *Speed*, it begins with the Dennis Hopper character; he is holding a group of hysterical office drones hostage in an elevator with bomb threats. At the end of that scene, ol' Dennis gets away—and you know he's not done terrorizing the good citizens of L.A.

In my Zebra Ballad release, *His Lady Bride*, I opened the book with Aric, my hero, seeking solitude, a respite from power, battle, and politics—only to be accosted by local villagers. They demand that Aric take a tempestuous, insult-spouting vixen to wife.

Faced with threats of her death, he marries her at the end of the scene, knowing all the while the inner peace he's spent so long building is forever gone. In that scene, you see Aric struggling immediately to accept the loss of his solitude. You see the anger he feels at this sudden union. And you see him trying his best to figure out what he's going to do with a completely unfamiliar wife who's calling him a fen-sucked lout.

I don't need to tell you that Aric needs peace more than he needs air, because I *showed* you why in the proceeding prologue. In that, I portrayed his guilt over the deaths of two young princes he believes he aided. He is disgusted with what his ambition has wrought, the utter carnage of common battle. I give you all this through a mix of character action, dialogue, and internal dialogue (what the character thinks to him/herself).

The inciting incident should set up the premise of your book so you can portray it in a way exciting to the reader. It should set up a dilemma in the reader's mind, a question that can only be answered by reading on. In *His Lady Bride*, readers will wonder what Aric will do without his peace—and what he will do with his bride.

The inciting incident should also give you enough story to write about for the next fourth of the book (about 100 pages in a long book, about 50 pages in a short one).

First turning point

Next, you'll want to plan the first turning point of your main plot. This is usually where the main character, who has likely been avoiding his/her problem since the beginning of the book, realizes that the problem won't go away and decides to face it. In *His Lady Bride*, Aric tries to maintain his distance from Gwenyth through several chapters. He does not want to get drawn into his very tempting wife's world and emotions.

But he finally realizes she is impossible to ignore. Not only are they irrevocably wed, he admires her spirit and finds himself needing to dry her tears after her unfeeling uncle casts her aside and her obnoxious cousin comes to gloat. His decision to accept what he cannot change enables him to plot a new course of action with Gwenyth, which propels the second quarter of the book.

Mid-point (second turning point)

The mid-point should be big! If you've ever read a book where you lost interest a little over halfway through, it's most likely because the writer did not have a strong mid-book event. At this point, your characters realize the problem is much deeper than they originally thought. In *Raiders of the Lost Ark*, Harrison Ford finds the Ark about halfway through the movie. He thinks his dreams are coming true: he's captured an important artifact, a worthy, exciting find.

But very quickly, he realizes the solution to his original problem— finding the Ark—comes with new and more frightening problems: Nazis, the wrath of God, near death, and the loss of his lady love.

This section of the book should hook the reader with a question: what will the character do in order to combat his new problem? This big event should not only entrance the reader, but should keep the action going for the next quarter of the book.

Third turning point

For the third turning point, we are ramping up toward the grand finale. It's here that your character realizes that he/she is the problem of the book. In other words, his/her own goals, wishes, plan, etc. are causing the strife. This is best depicted with a lot of action and dialogue. Again, you should leave the reader with a question, a sense of impending disaster.

In *His Lady Bride*, as the Wars of the Roses come to a violent and dramatic conclusion, Aric is forced to face his own issues with the past and his guilt. He feels certain that doom to his soul and honor are inevitable—unless he can find a way to face the past without damning either.

All seems well until he earns the king's displeasure. He suddenly finds himself facing a loss so profound, that it is likely to drive a wedge between him and Gwenyth forever.

Leaving this turning point, your reader should view this disaster as nearly insurmountable. The character should be so distraught and anguished about the event that it propels him/her directly into the crisis/black moment.

Crisis/black moment

For this crisis/black moment, an event (the crisis) occurs to compound the problems the character encountered during the third turning point. It must appear now as if all is lost, as if the character's obstacles to happiness will overwhelm him/her. Keep the scene looking bleak. Keep the reader in suspense, wondering until nearly the last page how such a crisis can be solved to everyone's satisfaction.

This brief, grim period (after the action of the crisis) is your "black moment."

Climax/resolution

This leads you to climax/resolution. During your climax, the action should unfold in such a way as to resolve the character's dilemmas, putting happiness back within his/her grasp. Be careful not to make this too simple or obvious. It's also best if this involves a change in the character, a realization that enables him to truly become a hero and deserve his happy ending.

The aftermath of the climax is the resolution. Here, your reader will see all the loose ends of your plot tied up, as your characters come to final resolution of all their problems.

In a romance, this is often where the characters admit their love and/or agree to marry. A good resolution is a bit like crossing your "t"s and dotting your "i"s—not completely necessary, but it makes any story richer and enhances the reader's understanding.

This is just a starting point on a complicated subject, but I hope it indicates a way to tackle those plot conundrums.

Best of luck in crafting your own successful plots!

CHAPTER 15

Characterization

Romeo and Juliet. Rhett and Scarlett. Why do certain characters (or pairs of characters, in romance novels) endure? What makes fictional people seem real to us? How can we as writers create characters that are just as realistic and compelling?

Before you start a story, you probably have a general idea about what sort of person you want to write about. Your heroine might be the girl-next-door or she might have a professional career. Your hero might be blue-collar or filthy rich. In other words, you've chosen wisely to create characters your readers can instantly recognize.

But to make these fictional people seem real, you must turn them from cookie-cutter stereotypes into living, breathing individuals. They should become people you care about as much as your best friends—so that your readers will care about them too.

Here are some techniques to help you flesh out characters.

Names

The first step is to give your characters a name. Maybe you've agonized over this, and well you should. Names have a lot to do with how a reader initially perceives a character.

A woman named Harriet gives the immediate impression of someone who is old-fashioned, and a man named Irving hardly sounds like a Chippendale's dancer. So put some thought into selecting the names you use.

In romance, heroes traditionally have strong, virile sounding names, while heroines' names tend to be softer. Still, if your heroine is a strong, aggressive woman, then a name like Scarlett might be just what you are looking for.

Learning the meaning of the names you choose can help define the personality aspects of your characters. Knowing Angeline means angel, you might feel moved to give that character angelic characteristics . . . or, just to be contrary, make her completely evil! It's up to you to decide how you will make use of a name (with its actual meaning and personal or literary associations). But that decision should never be arbitrary.

Physical traits also are important in the reader's perception of your characters. In romance, heroes and heroines are traditionally attractive people.

But does this mean they have to be perfect? Certainly not. Amanda Quick's heroines always have slight imperfections: buck teeth, weak eyes, a limp (not all in one character, of course!). By incorporating imperfections into her characters' make-up, she is able to create heroines her reader can identify with more easily.

Some traits are meant to be intriguing. A man with a scar is more interesting than one with a perfect face. The reader wonders how he got that scar and will keep reading to find out. A woman with soft hands indicates someone who's never had to work for a living.

So when describing your characters, choose physical traits that make them more interesting and lifelike to your readers.

Secondary characters

With secondary characters, physical traits play an even greater role. You can't spend the time with them to develop their background or engage them in dialogue that gradually shows their personality. So you'll need to give your readers visible clues about them.

Here, the question of stereotypes comes into play. Stereotypes can be especially useful (and appropriate) with secondary characters that don't need to be extremely complex.

A large or tall man conveys strength and power, while an extremely thin person might seem nervous and weak. If you can't devote a lot of time to a secondary character, consider letting the physical description do the talking for you.

Emotional Traits

Emotional traits are of utmost importance. Your characters' personalities and reactions will ultimately be key factors in keeping readers engaged in the story. Background plays a large part in determining this, but so do current phobias, mannerisms, and forms of speech.

Perhaps your heroine is afraid of the dark, likes to fidget with her rings when she is nervous, and has a favorite swearword. With just a few of these touches, your characters become more lifelike and memorable.

Emotional reactions should remain consistent throughout, with the exception of those scenes where your character is forced to confront their fears and beliefs. If the reader is first made aware that your heroine usually freezes in a crisis situation, then it is all the more dramatic when she is forced to take action.

Background

You should always know more about your characters' background than your readers. Have you ever had a person tell you their entire life story on a first date? If so, then you know how dull that can be—a case of too much information, too soon.

The same applies to your characters' background. If you attempt to describe their past lives all at once, then your readers' minds are going to wander. While flashbacks are sometimes necessary to explain a character's actions, keep this sort of exposition brief. Or better still, reveal the background through dialogue. Remember, it's not just what your hero and heroine say that reveal the keys to their characters, but what other people in the story say *about* them, as well.

But as the author, you need to be aware of your characters' backgrounds at all times. The past colors their thinking. And it should never be black and white.

Think shades of gray! Goody-goody heroes and thoroughly evil villains are one-dimensional. Let your hero have a bit of a dark side.

In the case of villains, they should either have some good in them, or else you should create something about them—perhaps a mitigating circumstance—that a reader can find a smidgen of sympathy for.

Create a background

How do you create a character's background? There are many methods, but I personally like to create an outline of the lives of my characters that occurs before the story—and work from there.

Here's a brief sample outline of a character background:

Justine Damaris was born and raised in New Orleans. When she was in her early teens, her mother died after a long fight with breast cancer. Her father, David, became distant after her mother's passing, even though Justine tried to win his attention by getting her private-eye license to become a partner in his detective agency.

She's intelligent, decisive, and always puts her father before herself. Her family history has left her feeling isolated and afraid of rejection. Because she fears rejection, she does not make friends easily and keeps her guard up at all times.

The first time she risks her heart for love, it is shattered. After she spends the night with the man of her dreams, Reed Burkett, he tells her they made a mistake.

Her emotional turmoil increases when her father runs up a string of gambling debts with a loan shark, then vanishes, leaving her to clean up his mess. Her worst fears have come true; she is truly alone . . . abandoned.

Reed Burkett re-enters her life to offer her a helping hand. Can she trust him after he broke her heart? Can she trust herself? Justine must somehow overcome her fears and doubts in order to find both her father and true love.

But some authors go way beyond that. J.R.R. Tolkien's long work *The Silmarillion*, consisting of hundreds of pages when finally published, was in many ways merely his extensive background notes for what became his greatest work, his *Lord of the Rings* trilogy!

Another method is to make up a questionnaire (see a sample of this at the end of this chapter, on pages 91-92). Fill out the questions as your character would. Where were you born and raised? What was your childhood like? Describe your current family and friends. Are you successful in maintaining these relationships? Are you religious?

In each case, instead of just answering yes or no, follow-up (as would a good interviewer) by asking for examples that show or explain the answer. By doing this, you can form a picture in your mind of your character's background and explore options for personality traits and quirks that would naturally develop from that person's experience.

Also, this method starts to give you a feeling for what the character understands about him or herself. This is valuable knowledge for you as an author, so that what you write is true to that person's point of view, so that it matches that person's self-awareness.

Furthermore, something in the character's "answers" to your questionnaire might provide ideas for how that character might grow during the course of the story—or how and why their perspective might come to change.

As you write, hold that characterization you've developed firmly in your mind. If you find your character challenged by a situation, go back to your outline or questionnaire and see if it offers clues to how the character might logically react.

Fully-developed characters have unique ways in which they interact with others and how they react in a given situation. For example, a woman raised in a convent might be shocked by a risqué anecdote or image, while a woman from a more liberal environment might simply appreciate and admire it.

The value of contrast

If you create a pair—a hero and heroine—with contrasting qualities, you set up a situation that allows the individual aspects of each personality to shine. An amiable hero with a surly heroine, or vice versa, allows you to play up their differences to their best advantage.

Also, the way your protagonists interact with secondary characters in your story can give the reader a good indication of their strengths and weaknesses.

Every scene is an opportunity

Just as every scene should do something to advance the plot, each scene should also give the reader greater insight into the characters' make-up.

Let the relationship between your characters and the reader develop as naturally as the relationship between the hero and heroine. It's a similar process of initial courtship, deepening involvement and admiration, and ultimate fulfillment.

Learn to listen

How do you know if you have created living breathing characters? This may sound crazy, but the best sign is if your characters start talking to you as you write!

And if you find yourself crying when they cry, so will your readers.

One last tip: if you do hear your characters talking to you, listen to what they have to say! They just might take your story in a direction you never dreamed of before.

Character Questionnaire

If you want to understand your characters, why not interview them? When you write down the responses to these questions, answer as if the character were speaking. Try to put yourself in their shoes.

- Where were you born and raised? What was your childhood like?

- Describe your family and childhood friends. Are you still close to them?

- Did you enjoy going to school? What were your favorite subjects?

- Did you graduate from high school? College? What impact has education had on your life?

- What is your religious background?

- Do you consider yourself a moral person?

- How far will you go to defend your convictions?

- Have you ever done anything you are ashamed of?

- What are your feelings about sex? How do these feelings affect your relationships?

- Are you an emotional person? Describe your temperament.

- Do have you have any phobias? Bad habits? Pet peeves?

- What do you look like? Are you happy with your appearance?

[cont. on next page]

Character Questionnaire (cont.)

- What is your most cherished possession? Why do you cherish it?

- Do you have any pets?

- Describe your current family and friends. Are you successful in maintaining these relationships?

- Do you have any enemies? Why do they oppose you?

- What is your occupation? Is it your dream job?

- What goal would you most like to achieve?

- What do you hope your life will be like in ten years?

CHAPTER 16

Hero Archetypes

by Caro LaFever

Beyond Alpha: Eight Male Archetypes

AS ROMANCE WRITERS, we spend a lot of time thinking about what kind of hero we want to create for our newest book. For years, we've heard of the alpha designation, along with the beta. Added to that have been the delta, the theta, and the subject of recent attention, the gamma.

But as I struggled to create a unique and exciting hero, I found myself confused by the different views I heard about each of these hero designations—especially the alpha. Some writers saw him as a natural leader, the man who everyone looks to for the answers. But others saw him as the rude, dominating hero that starred in many of the romances of the 70s—harsh, mean . . . even cruel.

And is the beta hero considerate and kind—or wishy-washy and complacent? Is the delta man merely a different kind of alpha? Is every tortured hero a theta? And what exactly is a gamma?

Some associates and I came to the conclusion that we needed to start from square one in thinking about heroes. The alpha/beta system had changed and grown so much, it was no longer useful. Many heroes did not fit any in of these categories. Trying to find the key to figuring out heroes, we discussed all the romance novels we'd read, besides viewing hundreds of movies and TV shows.

What we found surprised us. Heroes generally fall into eight clear archetypes. And this crossed all genres—romance, mystery, science fiction. The eight archetypes of heroes are instantly recognizable and have been used by writers from Shakespeare to Nora Roberts.

After much discussion, we labeled each hero archetype and went on to write a book titled *Heroes and Heroines: 16 Master Archetypes* by Caro LaFever, Tami Cowden, and Sue Viders. In our journey of discovery, we also identified eight heroine archetypes, which I'll present in the next chapter.

By defining and describing these archetypes, we were better able to pick and choose in our writing those characteristics that helped create exciting protagonists.

Here's an overview of what we found:

The Chief

Let's start with the *Chief*. For most romance writers, this is the quintessential alpha hero. Whether he's a born leader or a conqueror, this guy is tough, decisive and goal-oriented. He also can be overbearing and inflexible. Some examples of the *Chief* are John Wayne in most of his movies, Marlon Brando in *The Godfather* and Harrison Ford in *Sabrina*. His motto is "do something or get out of the way."

He's a leader, and people instinctively look to him for their answers. In his work life, he tends to rise to the top of his field. He could be a CEO of a major company—or in historical romances, a duke or prince.

Most romance heroes from the '70s and early '80s were *Chiefs*. Kathleen Woodiwiss's hero in *The Flame and the Flower* was a *Chief*. And this hero is still popular, starring in most Harlequin Presents books and Judith McNaught books.

Susan Elizabeth Phillips hero, Cal Bonner, in *Nobody's Baby But Mine* is a *Chief*.

The Bad Boy

Let's talk about the *Bad Boy*. Do you remember the guy in high school that was a little dangerous, but fascinating? The guy you dreamed about at night, but would have dropped dead with fright if he asked you out? This is the *Bad Boy*.

He could be a rebel without a cause, or the boy from the wrong side of the tracks. Either way, he's got a chip on his shoulder and a snarl on his face.

This hero is charismatic and street smart. He also can be bitter and volatile. He hates rules and regulations, and tends to cut his nose off to spite his face.

Patrick Swayze in *Dirty Dancing* or Matt Damon in *Good Will Hunting* are both *Bad Boys*. Jack Nicholson often plays this kind of hero. How about James Dean? Definitely a *Bad Boy*.

He's reckless, but inside he's got a vulnerable heart. This guy doesn't like bosses—he doesn't enjoy being told what to do. He stars in a lot of western romances; he's the perfect outlaw. Teresa Medeiros' hero in *Nobody's Darling* is a *Bad Boy*.

He also shows up in some Silhouette Intimate Moments as the man on the run.

The Best Friend

The *Best Friend* is another hero who's instantly familiar to most romance readers. This is the beta hero—the guy who's kind, decent, and responsible.

This is the kind of guy most women should probably marry in real life. He might be Mr. Nice Guy or the confidant you always tell your secrets to because he's invariably supportive and tolerant.

But he also can be unassertive and complacent. This guy doesn't enjoy confrontation and sometimes he gets stepped on because of it. Think of Jimmy Stewart in *It's a Wonderful Life*. Tom Hanks in almost any movie he does. Hugh Grant in *Four Weddings and a Funeral*. Or how about Bill Pullman in *While You Were Sleeping*?

In school, this guy went unappreciated until all the girls grew up and got smart. In romance novels, the *Best Friend* stars in a lot of Love and Laughters; light comedy seems to work well with this hero.

Many of LaVyrle Spencer's heroes are also *Best Friends*.

The Charmer

Ah, the *Charmer*. He's fun, irresistible and often unreliable. Give the *Charmer* a ball of twine and a few pieces of bread, and he magically creates a party.

This is the quintessential smooth operator. He might be a playboy or a rogue, but a woman cannot pin this guy down to any kind of commitment. Some examples of *Charmers* include Tom Selleck in *Magnum PI* or Eddie Murphy in *Beverly Hills Cop*.

Cary Grant always played a *Charmer*. And what about Leonardo Di-Caprio in *Titanic*?

This guy is attracted to occupations like salesman, newscaster, or gambler in the Wild West. He's not one for a lot of hard work. In romance, the *Charmer* stars in Susan Elizabeth Phillip's *Heaven, Texas* or *Lady Be Good*.

Again, light comedy works well with this hero, and so he easily stars in Duets and Harlequin Americans.

The Lost Soul

And now we come to the *Lost Soul*. In the old alphabet system, this would be your Theta hero. For centuries, he's had the starring role in a lot of plays and books. Think of Hamlet, and you've got a lock on this guy.

Tortured and secretive, he's got a vulnerable heart and discerning eyes. He also tends to brood to excess and can be unforgiving. He might wander through town, or maybe he was cast out because of some evil deed or physical deformity.

Good examples of the *Lost Soul* are Beast from *Beauty and the Beast* or David Duchovny from the *X-Files*. Nicholas Cage tends to play a lot of Lost Souls. Heathcliff from *Wuthering Heights* would be another good example.

In work, this man is very creative, but he's very much a loner, too—so he finds jobs like undercover cop or photographer. In historicals, he's the lone gunman.

Many heroes in Silhouette Intimate Moments are *Lost Souls*. Laura Kinsale and Mary Jo Putney also write *Lost Souls*.

The Professor

The *Professor*. At first glance, this is probably not your idea of a hero—at least not in romance novels. This guy is logical, introverted, and inflexible. But he's also genuine in his feelings. When he falls in love, it's for keeps. He's extremely faithful and honest.

Whether he's the absent-minded professor, like Woody Allen, or Mr. Organized, like Spock from *Star Trek*, he's a handy guy to have in your house when tax time rolls around. Sherlock Holmes is a perfect example of a *Professor*. Jeff Goldblum played one in *Independence Day*. And Kelsey Grammer's Frasier is also a *Professor*.

At work, this guy likes numbers, data, and hard cold facts. He's meticulous and an expert in his field. In historicals, he's the hero finding dinosaur bones or researching the Renaissance. Jayne Ann Krentz's heroes are fabulous *Professors*, as are Amanda Quick's.

Also, pairing a professor with a ditzy heroine can be very funny—as Colleen Collins did in *Right Chest, Wrong Name*, a popular Harlequin Love and Laughter.

The Swashbuckler

And now we come to the *Swashbuckler*. This hero is a man on the go. Action, action, and more action is his motto. He is physical, daring, and mercurial.

If you stay around him for long, you'll be sucked into his whirlwind. He's capable of getting himself into trouble, but also of finding his way out of the trap.

He could be a daredevil, in it for the adrenaline rush. Or he could be an explorer, reaching toward a specific goal. Think of Indiana Jones, Jackie Chan, Zorro. Or how about Will Smith in *Men in Black*? All these guys share a common energy and enormous courage.

Occupations that lure this man are ones like smoke jumper, investigative journalist, and astronaut—anything with thrills and chills involved. Karen Robards often creates this type of hero.

And if you love pirates, then you must love *Swashbucklers*.

The Warrior

Last, but not least, comes the *Warrior*. This is the old delta hero—the reluctant rescuer. He's dark and dangerous, driven and remote. But if there's a damsel in distress, he's your man.

Maybe he's avenging an injustice done to him or his family. Or perhaps he's the knight in shining armor, a patriot through and through. Either way, he's always noble, tenacious, and relentless.

There are tons of examples of this kind of hero in the movies. Dirty Harry. Steven Seagal. Chuck Norris. And Bruce Willis in *Die Hard*.

If it doesn't fit his moral code, this guy will walk away from the job. He won't play the game just to get along. He's the FBI agent or the Navy SEAL.

Susan Brockman has made a career writing about this type of hero. Also, many of Linda Howard's heroes are *Warriors*.

This list should help you see that there are more kinds of heroes than you may realize to explore and write about. In the next chapter, we'll look at some female archetypes.

Put the right combination together, and you've got a story that will sparkle with real energy.

CHAPTER 17

Heroine Archetypes

by Caro LaFever

Beyond Cinderella: Eight Female Archetypes

BEING A ROMANCE WRITER, I naturally spend quite a bit of time thinking about men. What is appealing about one man over another? What qualities do I want the one I'm creating to possess?

Sometimes, in my search for the perfect hero, I tend to forget my poor, overlooked heroine. I spend so much effort creating my hero, I find myself with less time to bring my heroine to life.

I think this is true of many romance writers. On and on we talk in endless discussion about heroes. What type is he? Why did he become this way.

I've never seen such an equal discussion of heroines. The differing kinds of women it's possible to create never seem to stir the same fervor in romance writers that the men do.

But why not? Isn't it equally as important to explore the varied female characteristics available—now that we've moved past the classic damsel in distress?

After spending hours with my critique group discussing romance novels (and movies and TV shows), we came to a startling discovery: heroines are as important to a good story as heroes. And there are clearly defined differences in heroines—enough that a consideration of just one or two categories didn't cover the field.

In fact, heroines generally fall into eight clear archetypes. And this crosses all genres—romance, mystery, science fiction. The eight heroine archetypes are instantly recognizable to most writers. They just haven't been defined and talked about in as much detail as heroes have.

After much discussion, we labeled each heroine archetype that we found and included these in our book *Heroes and Heroines: 16 Master Archetypes* by Caro LaFever, Tami Cowden, and Sue Viders.

Here's a brief overview of the different heroines, with some hints for how you can use them as you create your own versions in your stories:

The Boss

First, let's talk about the *Boss*. A "take charge" woman, she's outspoken and persuasive. Goals and winning are important, and she doesn't care how many feathers she ruffles to get ahead. She might be accustomed to winning since birth.

Or she might have had to fight her way to the top. But this woman never gives up until she's on top of the heap.

Think of Candace Bergen as Murphy Brown or Cate Blanchette as Queen Elizabeth. Like all *Bosses*, both are confident, competitive, and arrogant. They tend to be workaholics because they operate in fields that have clear-cut goals, where achievement is rewarded. They're efficient managers, but are demanding of their co-workers and underlings. If you don't watch out, she'll run you down.

Jennifer Greene in her book, *200% Wife*, shows a *Boss* trying to change in a typical *Boss* way.

The Seductress

On to the *Seductress*. She slinks into the room, beguiling the men and offending the women. She's mysterious and manipulative.

Underneath her wiles, she's got a streak of distrust a mile wide and ten miles deep. Her cynical view of life rules her actions—she'll never be left holding the bill. Her strong sense of survival means she's willing to do whatever is necessary to come out ahead.

Sharon Stone in *Basic Instinct* played one of these women. Or think of Madonna in *Evita*. How about Vivian Leigh in *Gone With the Wind*?

She might edge close to being the villain of a story. Or maybe she fell into using her personal allure as a weapon. Either way, this woman always lands on her feet. Independent and clever, she does well in jobs that exploit her charms—a spy or a model.

She carefully hides her intelligence behind a charming smile. Nora Robert's heroine in *Daring to Dream* is a *Seductress*.

The Spunky Kid

Okay, then there's the *Spunky Kid*. Spirited and loyal, this heroine is a favorite of many romance writers. She's got moxie, but she doesn't need to be on top of the corporate ladder. Instead, she finds her own niche, as ace reporter or owner of the coffee shop next door.

A good sense of humor carries her through many a trial in her love life—she tends to be the eternal bridesmaid. She finds it much easier to play ball with the guys, rather than put on those painful stiletto heels and vamp. Reliable and supportive, she makes friends wherever she goes.

Mary Tyler Moore as Mary Richards was the quintessential *Spunky Kid*. Whoopi Goldberg in *Sister Act* or Sandra Bullock in *While You Were Sleeping* were both *Spunky Kids*.

On the job, she mediates problems with compassion and fairness, but finds it hard to say "no" to a pleading face. She's the secretary who the boss overlooks or the girl next door who never gets recognized as a woman.

Judith McNaught's heroine in *Whitney, My Love* is a classic *Spunky Kid*.

The Free Spirit

Genuine and fun-loving, the *Free Spirit* skips through life, always expecting the best result. She's impulsive and because of this, a handful for those who get involved with her. She's an "original" and a trendsetter, never willing to settle for the ordinary.

She might be the zany comedian who brings life to every party. Or maybe she's the darling of her clan, who leaves a trail of good intentions behind her.

Think of Lucille Ball and you've got a lock on this gal. How about Alicia Silverstone in *Clueless* or Jenna Elfman from *Dharma & Greg*? Both of these ladies share the same sincerity and imagination as well as an impulsive need to meddle in their friends' lives.

A *Free Spirit* gravitates to careers that allow her to express herself—fashion designer, florist, or musician. She might be that beautician who decided you needed a punk hairdo—and somehow, convinced you it was perfect.

Jayne Ann Krentz (aka Amanda Quick) uses her *Free Spirit* heroines to humorous affect in all of her books.

The Waif

And now, the *Waif*. This classic damsel in distress is the star of many fairy tales we grew up with. She's Cinderella and Sleeping Beauty and Rapunzel all rolled into one. Her child-like innocence calls out for protection and rescue. She's naïve and docile.

Everyone she meets wants to save her. But she can surprise people with her strength of will. The *Waif* doesn't fight back; instead, she endures. Fay Wray in *King Kong* is a *Waif*. Audrey Hepburn often played this heroine—think of *Sabrina*. Or what about Robin Wright in *The Princess Bride*?

All of these women are pure, trusting, insecure. They seem to be untouched by the world, patient, and able to adapt to any situation.

In work, this heroine rarely seeks out a particular job. She seems to fall into whatever position she finds herself in. Everyone around her underestimates her resiliency, but her need to please others can prove a powerful motivation.

The *Waif* starred in almost all early romances— think of Kathleen Woodiwiss's heroine in *The Flame and the Flower*.

The Librarian

The *Librarian* is no man's fantasy woman, right? She's conscientious, orderly, and bright. Because of this, she leads with her brain, not her looks. Somewhere in her childhood, she learned that physical charms shouldn't—or couldn't—help her get ahead.

She might be the know-it-all who always remembers the answer. Or on the other hand, she could be the shy mouse hiding in the corner.

Shelly Long in Cheers played a *Librarian*. Or think of Gillian Anderson in the *X-Files* or Kathleen Turner in *Romancing the Stone*. Each of these women is serious and efficient, but also rigid and repressed.

In work, this heroine is attracted to jobs that deal with information instead of people. She could be an accountant or a chemist. Facts are what she depends on, and her stubborn refusal to look at another side can often spell trouble.

Silhouette Desires and Harlequin Temptations use the sexual awakening of *Librarians* in many of their stories.

The Crusader

Now we come to the *Crusader*. She marches into the room, intent on her mission. Tenacious and headstrong, she despises any opposition to her goal. Don't try to calm her down or divert her to going on a picnic. She'll brush right past you. She's got no time to waste with trivialities.

Sigourney Weaver in *Alien* was a quintessential *Crusader*. Other heroines that fit this description are Sarah Michelle Gellar in *Buffy the Vampire Slayer* and Helen Hunt in *Twister*. These women have enormous courage, are persuasive in trying to win people to their cause, and are obstinate in the face of failure.

She gravitates to jobs that make a difference—environmental activist or FBI agent. Until the battle is won, she'll never lay down her arms.

Think of romantic suspense—Harlequin Intrigue—and you'll find many *Crusaders*.

The Nurturer

Finally, we come to the *Nurturer*. A wonderful listener, pleasant and enjoyable to be around, this heroine takes care of everyone. She's serene, capable, and optimistic.

She might be the laid-back mother who always has fresh cookies in the oven. Or she might be bound by duty and love, always caring for her family and friends with steely determination.

Michelle Pfeiffer in *Ladyhawk* played a *Nurturer*. Other examples are Renee Zellweger in *Jerry Maguire* or Phylicia Rashad in *The Bill Cosby Show*.

This woman is altruistic to a fault; others' needs always come before her own. She's the calm mentor who guides her charges to a successful future, or the wise woman who knows all the answers.

At work, she's happiest in occupations that allow her to serve and care for others—paramedic, social worker, defense lawyer. Eternally optimistic, she's the rock on which her family and friends stand.

Nurturers work well in family-based stories—check out Silhouette Special Editions and Harlequin SuperRomances.

CHAPTER 18

Internal Conflict

by Shelley Bradley

OH, NO. You've opened your mailbox to discover your latest rejection letter. Or the contest score sheet which again cites your lack of the fictional element that makes you want to drive off a cliff at its mere mention: Internal Conflict.

Okay, before you run shrieking from your computer, take a deep breath and relax. We're going to get through this.

Definition

Let's start easy. I define internal conflict as "a moral or belief firmly held by a protagonist that *directly clashes* with a moral or belief firmly held by an opposing character."

For example, your heroine is the kind of woman who each day quietly hums "We've Only Just Begun." But your hero prefers to shout the lyrics to "Love Stinks." Why? Because she believes that love heals, while he feels certain that love destroys. Their beliefs are in complete opposition.

Be careful here. Make certain this conflict isn't something the hero and heroine can solve in a conversation or two. For instance, let's create a fictional hero who hates women who lie. If the hero assumes that the heroine is lying to him about the ranch (for whatever reason)—but in fact, she isn't—and they are too busy arguing to have a real conversation, that is not internal conflict. That is a misunderstanding.

Yes, he has a moral stance against lying. However, there is no opposing belief from the heroine.

Now, let's make our hero a gambler—and our heroine a preacher's widow. If she were indeed intentionally lying about the ranch (despite a bruised conscience), to keep that drifting cheat of a hero, the kind of man who killed her husband, from taking over her ranch and leaving her children homeless . . . that is internal conflict.

It's not so hard to see the difference. The simplicity of internal conflict lies in its motivation, which *must* be a part of the character's life experience.

You can't just pluck a belief out of the air and expect to carry that through the book with any conviction. If you do, you're likely to have editors or judges say, "Well, why doesn't she like Frenchmen?" If your only answer is that her mother told her not to, then that's not only prejudicial, but weakly motivated.

An Example

Only You, a novel by Elizabeth Lowell, offers a spectacular example of motivation. In it, Lowell's fictional hero, Matt "Reno" Moran tells the heroine Eve, "You can't count on women, but you can count on gold." He has come to believe this because his former fiancée left him to wed another, much older man, deciding to secure her comfort rather than follow Reno into the untamed West.

The author takes it a step further, however, by opening the book at a poker game, in which the heroine Eve bets herself. She then deals Reno (then a total stranger) the winning hand.

When accusations of cheating erupt around the table, Eve scoops up the pot and flees, leaving Reno behind to fight a band of cutthroats.

This confirms Reno's belief that Eve is like his one-time lady-love, Savannah—she can't really care for anyone but herself. In his mind, Eve is even worse because she not only used her body to tease him with no intention of paying up, as did Savannah, but she also abandoned him to potentially die in a gunfight.

Reno also believes that since women have no heart for others, he'll never find one who will give herself purely in passion, without using sex as bait for marriage or declarations of love.

Eve, on the other hand, has never really known love and wants it desperately. Sold from an orphan train to an elderly couple, she grew up in an environment where the old couple did little to foster her—except teach her to cheat at cards and lecture her on the evil of men's carnal desires.

When she realizes she must become Reno's lover to honor her ante at the poker game—yet not wanting to become another ruined woman he will simply use and leave—Eve resists the sensual temptation that Reno presents.

The resultant sparks created as Eve and Reno work through these conflicts give the book its story depth, character revelation, and great sexual tension.

Internal and External Conflicts

The more motivated a moral belief is in each character's experience, the more firmly the character will hold it. And the more firmly they hold it, the more able you are as a writer to draw from that well throughout the book for conflict.

What does that mean, you ask? Learn to play your internal conflict cards in every chapter—by making your external conflict exacerbate the internal one.

In *Only You*, Eve and Reno end up sharing a map to an old Jesuit gold mine. They must work together to discover the mine's location (after it has rested undisturbed for nearly three hundred years). This situation is rife with ways for each character to explore the reasons for their distrust of each other.

Repeatedly, you see the push-pull that adds chemistry to the characters and zing to the sexual tension—all because they have something both important and firmly believed in to argue about.

Point and Counterpoint

That's all well and good, but how do you explore the internal conflict further? This is where it gets tricky. Too many writers end up talking more about the external and forget everything else.

Here's a tip. Screenwriters use something called *Point and Counterpoint*. What is this? In simple terms, it's creating situations throughout the book that alternately prove and disprove (or challenge) your hero and heroine's beliefs.

The other juicy effect of this technique is that it develops internal conflict within the character himself. He begins to wonder if perhaps he's been wrong, possibly too harsh. Then, just when he's vacillating, you give him another story reason to cling to his belief, though maybe in a slightly altered way. So the conflict is back.

Putting it all together

If you use all these techniques, you have an internal clash between your hero and heroine, an external reason to argue, and each character fighting within him/herself for the truth. This gives you good pacing and story depth.

Are you still having trouble with internal conflict? Here's a simple solution, what I call the "cheater's way." First, settle on an external conflict. Then, decide on opposing internal beliefs for both your hero and heroine that fit within the context of that external conflict.

Once you have all that, then you can decide how you can resolve their internal conflict. In other words, explore in advance what will make each of the characters change their minds.

Perhaps you put your characters in a situation that forces them to behave in the very manner they've been criticizing. Or put them in a situation in which they realize (hopefully by virtue of the unfolding resolution of the external conflict) that they've been wrong. However it's best for you, decide *up front* how your characters will complete their arc and come to change. Once that you've done that, *then* plug in the life experience that logically gives each character his or her motivation for the belief.

It's a simple series of steps that will help your story immensely.

Wrapping it up

Now that you have all that down and you've plugged it into your story, deliver the satisfying ending. In your story, *put the resolution of your internal conflict last.* Let the hero and heroine complete their character arcs during the black moment, decide the fate of the ranch somewhere around there . . . and then, declare their love for each other at the *end* the book.

Toward the end of *Only You*, Eve and Reno discovered the gold mine. This resolves the external-conflict question. But as they work together to bring the gold out of the mine, part of it collapses. Reno is trapped inside.

Eve knows she alone does not possess the strength to rescue him, and she plots instead to barter the gold to save Reno's life. Meanwhile, Reno's friends ride to her aid instead. Still, although they help her to free Reno, ultimately Eve is the only person small enough to crawl through the hole dug into that part of the mine.

But after she frees Reno, he only hears that she tried to plot with his enemy; he refuses to believe she had altruistic motives. Believing Reno will never love or trust her, Eve rides away. She tells him that she left behind his gold, since he could count on it.

The author completes the hero's character arc during his black moment when he realizes that Eve was willing to risk both her gold and her life to save him. He knows then he was wrong and that he found a woman he can trust.

The resolution of the internal conflict comes about when Reno tracks Eve down. In a great twist, she is wearing the same saloon girl's garb she wore in the book's opening. But this time she is alone. Reno apologizes and confesses his love, then offers to leave Eve alone, if that is her wish.

In this last emotional moment, the author touches us with the depth of Reno's character arc—and satisfies us with the emotional resolution of the internal conflict. We put the book down with a sigh because the author created the need for emotional payoff, then saved it for last.

Now that you know how and why . . . you can, too.

CHAPTER 19

Finding Your Voice

VOICE IS AN ELUSIVE QUALITY. But elusive or not, it's a quality that editors look for more than anything else. Best-selling authors have very distinct voices. If someone handed me one of their books without their names on them, I could identify the writing of Nora Roberts, Julie Garwood, Linda Howard, and others of their caliber.

An author's voice is not so much about *what* you write as *how* you write and how it sounds to the reader. What is your style: formal or informal? What is the rhythm of your story? Does it flow? Does it have a lilt? Or is it fast-paced and abrupt, with many stops and starts?

Voice has a lot to do with whether or not your story *speaks* to the reader. Think of yourself as a storyteller. Does the way you tell your story make it obvious who you are, so that if they closed their eyes (or in the case of a writer, hid the name on the front cover and title page of your book), your audience would know you . . . by your voice?

I've read many good books by excellent writers that I didn't really like, mostly because the writer's voice bothered me in some indefinable way. Have you ever had this happen to you? Everybody raves about a book. You read it—and have an opposite reaction. Voice is the personal connection between writer and reader. If the connection isn't there, then odds are the reader won't enjoy the story.

In their quest to write a marketable story, new writers often work hard—often too hard—to make their stories perfect. They go over their first chapter again and again, taking out anything that they think an editor wouldn't like. The problem is that in their quest to be perfect, they often take out the very thing that makes their writing unique: their voice.

The new writer is afraid that those little quirky turns of phrase, those unexpected descriptions, don't quite fit with "perfect" writing. But if they are you and you take them out, you could be in danger of losing your voice.

My speaking voice has a southern accent. It can't be helped, since I was born and raised in Florida and now live in Texas. It makes sense that my writing voice, no matter what period or setting I'm writing in, always has a *tinge* of the south in there too. I'm not talking about character dialects, although I'll allow it's easier for me to write dialogue for southern characters.

The southern tinge shows up in the kind of humor I use—the informal and loose style, the pacing of my narrative and dialogue, the little phrases like "before God and everybody" that I tend to use.

But it's more than that. It's not just all "deep south" in there, because part of the voice is just me and how my mind works. It reflects my individual voice—my own background and thoughts and experiences. These are harder to categorize than a regional accent, that might be more widespread and therefore recognizable. But my voice is all of those, wrapped up in a package that's just, well, little ol' me. It's how I write.

It takes a lot of honesty and courage to expose yourself in your writing this way. But to find your voice is exactly what you need to do.

Finding your voice

I don't think voice is something you can create. It's more something that just *is*. But you can learn to recognize it, and encourage it to grow.

It should flow naturally from you. I didn't find my voice right away. It sort of gradually came out as I gained confidence as a writer. When I read my earlier books, I can see glimmers of it here and there. But I can also see where I thought the story sounded too folksy or something . . .

and I edited it into something more formal. Stilted. Flat. Something that wasn't me. I took that "sparkle" out of there. But sparkle is exactly what editors want, and look for, and do little dances of joy when they find it.

Here's a tip. Do you keep a journal or diary? (You should. It's a good thing to do as a writer.) Pull it out and open it up to a recent page. Put it next to a page or two from your current manuscript. And compare your journal entries with your writing.

Read the two aloud. The two don't need to match; journal writing is different from fiction writing. But how different do they sound? And the most important question is: can you hear yourself in your fiction writing? Even if you are writing in another time period, you should be able to hear your voice.

Write with confidence

Once you find your voice and start writing without thinking about working with the safety net of "perfect" writing, your life might become a whole lot easier and your writing might get stronger. You stop questioning every word you put on the page and simply get down to the business of telling your story.

By writing without that persnickety "internal editor" on, you'll increase your productivity and be able to write more . . . and faster.

Yes, you'll still need to edit afterwards. Even the great authors with their wonderful voices still know they need to do that.

But that's better than questioning and editing every word you put down as you write. While critique groups are great for feedback and for finding ways to improve your story, be sure you always listen to the advice with your "voice filter" on.

Learn to recognize when a comment is a question of voice, compared to other issues of effective or ineffective writing.

Don't let the voices of others silence yours.

Some people might not connect with your voice. So what? Think of the people who will. And write for them. Think about how your voice makes your work unique

Because only you can sound like you.

Section 3

Support Networks

CHAPTER 20

Successful Critiquing

OR A NEW WRITER, submitting work for critique can be excruciating. It needn't be. Just keep in mind these three little words: *It Ain't Gospel*. So "ain't" isn't proper English. See? You've critiqued me already. And I don't even mind! I've always found those three words comforting, and so have people I've critiqued in turn.

What the phrase means is: the opinions you are given are suggestions . . . not commandments.

Consider them carefully, but feel free to disregard what doesn't work for you. Remember, this is *your* story. You have the final say about what stays and what goes.

Feel better now? Good. Now that you're ready to be critiqued, the first thing to do is find somebody to critique you. Whatever method you use to find a partner, whether online or by joining a local critique group, realize that you'll need to prepare to *give* critiques as well as receive them. In most cases, unless you are paying for a critiquing service, you'll be expected to reciprocate the favor.

I hear some of you out there wailing, "But . . . I'm a *new* writer! Why would anybody want an opinion from *me*?"

Look, if you can read and write, then you can give a critique. You know what you like, right? All that is required is to honestly tell your partner what does and doesn't work for you.

Ground Rules

It is, however, a good idea to lay down some ground rules before you start. Find out what your partner or group expects from a critique. Do they want a line-by-line edit for errors of technique? Or would they prefer to hear your impressions about plot and character?

How in-depth should you go? Determine the kind of help your writing colleagues want right from the start. It avoids hassles and misunderstandings later on.

The same goes for you when you submit your work for review. You might wish to tell your partner ahead of time about any points you are particularly worried about or feel might be weak, so they can give those areas special attention. But don't go on and on—you want them to read the work and form their own impressions.

If you're working with a local group (or even an online partner), consider drawing up a simple "contract." Set a time limit for how long you will work together, with an option to renew when that initial period has expired. This way, if the critiquing is not working out, it leaves the disenchanted parties with the ability to back out with no questions asked.

Decide where, when, and how often you'll meet. But keep things flexible. There will be times when you can't make a meeting. If so, let your partners know in advance so they can consider rescheduling if they wish.

Discuss the agenda of your meetings. Set limits on each person's critiquing time. If you are going to read passages of each others work aloud (which I recommend), set a timer. This way, everyone has a chance to get their work reviewed, and no one will leave feeling their work didn't get enough attention.

If you're working online or via mail, set a response time. Again, if for some reason you can't make the deadline, let your partner know in advance.

Work out how many pages will be critiqued at a time. Will it be chapter-by-chapter? Scene-by-scene? Don't hand over an entire manuscript unless someone asks for it.

By laying down these ground rules in advance, your meetings should be more productive.

Giving a critique

I'm often asked how to give a critique. This is a hard question to answer because every critique should be suited to the person's needs. My main rule is always find something positive to say.

Lead off your comments with the positive—and end that way, too. Yes, a critique should point out flaws, but it needs to give a writer some real encouragement, too.

I feel it's best if you read through the entire selection before you begin critiquing, to familiarize yourself with the person's style, plot, and characters. This also helps to avoid raising early questions that prove to be answered later in the story.

If your partner wants a "line edit" (i.e., going over the work sentence-by-sentence), then focus on technique first. Look for POV changes, bad sentence structure, grammar or formatting problems.

For POV, I find it helps if you draw brackets that mark the changes, stating whose POV is active within each bracketed segment. Another way to do this is to use different color highlighters. But just saying "Watch for POV changes" is little help. *Show them* where you think the POV shifts, and even better yet, write a note that says *why* you think it shifts.

Do the same with bad sentence structure. If possible, rewrite the sentence to show them how you think it should read. But, please, be gentle. I usually make my comments read, "Would something like this work?" Remember, you're only giving suggestions.

For grammar or formatting matters, however, it's important they follow the basic rules. So if you find something wrong, just say so.

If your partner wants a "general" critique (i.e., looking more at an overview of how well the story works), concentrate on the plot and characters. Are the heroine and hero likable? Does the plot flow coherently? Is the pacing too fast or too slow? Does the dialogue sound forced or natural? Is the conflict believable?

You'll be surprised how often the answers will jump right off the pages for you—a fresh, outside reader—when you ask these questions. If you're asked to look for specific problems, be sure to do so. Try your best to give your partners the feedback they need.

After you've shared your comments, if the writer disagrees with you, do *not* take it personally. Don't try to force your opinions on them.

Remember, *it ain't gospel*.

You did your job. It's up to the writer to decide whether or not they choose to use your suggestions.

Receiving a critique

The first rule is: shut up and listen!

Yes, there's a natural tendency to want to defend your work. (I have this tendency myself, so I know exactly how you feel.) But instead, bite your tongue and don't interrupt, *even if you feel the comments are unfair*. Of course, if someone asks you a question to clarify something, answer it. Otherwise, be quiet. And *listen*!

I can't emphasize this enough. It's natural for you to get defensive about it, or for your attention to wander, if you hear things you don't want to hear. But remember, these people are trying to help you, right? If they went to the trouble to read your work and comment on it, the least you can do is listen respectfully.

Next, you need to begin to filter through the information. In a group situation, it's possible to receive conflicting opinions. Don't just agree with the ones you like. Consider each comment carefully before you throw yourself into a rewrite. And keep the comments in mind as you revise to avoid making the same mistakes.

Even if you don't agree with a suggestion, acknowledge that there may be an underlying problem with a piece of your writing that caused that reader to feel the need to make that suggestion in the first place. Even if the solution proposed isn't the right one, that person may have pointed out a problem that needs addressing.

And in general, you'll know when critiques hit their mark. You'll get that sense—a feeling deep inside that, yes, you know exactly what they mean. It matches up with something you already know, but perhaps couldn't articulate or put your finger on. You'll start to imagine a way to fix what they've indicated rubs them the wrong way.

It could also be something you knew was a little weak, but just thought you could get away with—maybe no one would notice. Well, guess what . . . they did, and they called you on it.

If you're receiving critiques via a written medium, read through the comments once. Set them aside. And then read them again . . . later. Why? I recommend this because often the negative comments hit people so hard that they tend to overlook the good things people say.

By taking time to digest and review the information, you'll get a clearer picture of what your critiquer is trying to say.

Rewards and Pitfalls

I've had my work critiqued in just about every way possible. I've entered contests that offered written feedback from judges. I've had an e-mail partner, a snail-mail partner. I've joined online groups and a local one of my RWA chapter.

Each experience was rewarding. Each person brought their own perspectives to the dance. I can't think of a single instance where I didn't learn something new.

On the other hand, there are pitfalls you shouldn't ignore. If your partner only gives you glowing reviews, that's a problem. And the same is true if all the feedback you get is negative.

There needs to be a balance. And there needs to be trust. It might take some time before you feel comfortable enough with your group to be completely honest. Bear in mind, your partners might feel the same way. So take it one suggestion at a time and see what happens.

Occasionally, you'll run across someone whose personality doesn't mesh well with yours. Personality clashes can result in unfair critiques. And yes, there are people who feel so insecure about themselves, they "nuke" everybody else's stuff in an effort to feel superior. This is why I recommended a time limit for critiques. It gives you a graceful way to stop a single person's rant and move on to the next person ... who likely will find something especially fair and kinder to say in reaction to the overblown comments just offered.

For a new writer, though, this kind of negative experience can be devastating. While that's understandable, you shouldn't let it discourage you from sharing your work. Critiquing is a give-and-take process, and hearing a variety of opinions is the norm. One way or another, everyone is trying to help you improve your writing. Most writers have the tact and the empathy to present their opinions in a constructive, caring manner.

Your critique partners are there to help you—and to get help from you in return. That's what critiquing is all about. It might take some searching on your part to find the perfect partner. But trust me, the rewards make it well worth the search.

Just remember, *it ain't gospel.*

CHAPTER 21

The Benefits of Contests

WHEN AND WHY should a writer enter a contest? There are several reasons. Consider both the details of the contest itself and where you are in your writing career to determine which reason or reasons best apply to you.

Most writing contests clearly state what the entrant can expect from their guidelines. These guidelines give the entrant the information they need to decide whether or not it is worth their while to pay the entrance fee—assuming there is one.

Romance writers have a good variety of contest choices available, since many local RWA chapters sponsor a contest every year. But if you keep an eye out, you'll also find writing contests sponsored by romance magazines and romance book publishers.

Entrance fees vary. With contests sponsored by RWA chapters, you might need to be a RWA member to enter; other contests allow non-members to enter—sometimes at a higher fee. Double-check contest guidelines, which are usually posted on chapters' websites. Publishers' contests often do not charge fees to enter, but again this varies.

The guidelines should also state whether the contest judges will provide feedback, which romance subgenres are included, manuscript format information, length of submissions, and contest deadlines. If you have questions, don't hesitate to contact the sponsors for more information.

A new writer should look for contests that give written feedback. These are critiques—critiques that you pay for with your entrance fee. In most case, the judges will be published authors or experienced writers on the brink of being published. These judges can give you valuable (and impartial) advice on how to improve your work.

If you yourself are an experienced writer—perhaps you've submitted work and received positive encouragement in rejection letters—then look especially for contests that include editors as the finalist judges or contests that include the submission or even publication of your manuscript if it is a top prize-winner. Many emerging writers have had their winning submissions published this way and have been noticed by editors seeking new talent. Who knows? It could happen to you, too.

For published authors, contests provide promotional opportunities as well as validation for their work. It doesn't hurt to have a few award credits to add to your bio next time you mail a query to an editor, does it?

The two most prestigious contests for romance writers are RWA National's Golden Heart (for unpublished writers) and RITA award (for published authors). While the Golden Heart does not usually supply any feedback beyond contest scores, many Golden Heart winners and finalists have gone on to have their books published. For more information, visit this RWA link: http://rwanational.org/ContestMenu04.htm.

Remember, for most contests, the judges change every year. So work overlooked one year may easily win a big prize the next. Don't give up just because you don't get noticed your first time out. Review feedback, if any, and consider the odds. You may want to resubmit the same material to the same contest the next year or to a similar one. Just because one judge didn't respond to your story doesn't mean you don't have a winner—if submitted to the right contest in the right year.

CHAPTER 22

On Contests

by Liz Flaherty

I T'S HARD TO BE IN THIS BUSINESS without learning something about contests and how they are judged. Before you're done, you will have entered contests or judged contests or, if you're like many of us, you will have done both. I've been at it since I entered my first contest in 1994.

It was my very first manuscript, and I won First Place. I thought, *Well, I'll be published by the end of the year and can quit my day job and start painting my toenails in preparation for appearances on Oprah, Sally, and Phil.*

Ahem. Four years and several contests later, I was still unpublished. I'm still working my day job. I only polished my toenails for my son's wedding. And Phil Donahue gave up on me and retired (oh, he of little faith!)

But I've learned things. Oh, boy, have I learned things! And yes, in the process, I've had several of my works published

Along the way, I've learned that if you're thin-skinned, entering contests is not a particularly good idea. The prize in my aforementioned first contest was a full-scale critique by an RWA chapter far away. None of the members of this chapter knew me, none cared how many hours I'd spent on *The Growing Season*, none knew my skin was thin enough to be broken by a stiff breeze.

What they knew was that my POV sucked, my conflict was nonexistent, my hero was weak, my heroine unattractive. The book had too many kids and too many shopping scenes. And I didn't know what I was talking about when it came to the subject matter.

Quite literally, I sat on the couch with the 13 critiques from the chapter far away and tears rolled stingingly over skin that had just been broken wide open by the cold wind of criticism.

After a month or two had passed, during which time I didn't write a single word, I hauled out the critiques and read them again. Yeah, my POV was bad . . . but my hero was okay. He was no alpha guy, for sure, but I don't even like alpha guys.

I did need more conflict, but the kids were good as they were. Yes, I could easily dump a shopping scene. The subject matter? Well, I did know what I was talking about—I'd been there.

The unattractive heroine? Four years later, that remark still hurts because my first heroine in my first book was, of course, me.

I entered *The Growing Season* in the Golden Heart contest. I didn't reach the finals, but I had good scores and received wonderful, helpful remarks from the judges.

The comments weren't all positive, but they were written in ways that did not abrade my still-scabby skin. They were presented as opinions, from people who, even though they didn't know me, understood I'd spent a lot of time on my manuscript and deeply cared about it. And the comments were written in "what if . . ." style. I only remember a few of their names, but I am eternally grateful to them.

Shirley Karr shared this story. "In a well-known contest, one of the judges ripped an author's manuscript apart for 'factual errors.' The scene in discussion took place on a plane. The judge wrote at great length, in less than kind terms, about how the author had obviously not done her research because anyone who flew knew that a Boeing *XXX* had such-and-such layout. Nothing at all like what that author described in her story.

"The author's day job? Flight attendant, often on a Boeing *XXX*."

Karr recalled another story, though, that shows the full range of judges' willingness to help contestants improve their work. "On the flip side, one of my critique partners, Jan, was judging in a contest, the historical category. The entrant described the hero's Levi jeans, but it didn't sound quite right to Jan.

"Being an apparel manager at a department store, Jan called the Levi hotline and got the facts on Levis as manufactured in the year in question. She wrote this info on the score sheet, and included the 800 number so the writer could verify or ask other questions. The entrant sent Jan a gushing thank-you note."

So what can we learn from these stories and the others we often hear, describing the ups and downs of contests?

If you're going to enter contests:

1. Develop a thick skin. Develop a thick skin. This is worth saying twice. I can't get back that month of productivity I lost back in 1994.

2. Send thank-you notes—even if you have to wait until your blood pressure goes down to write them.

3. Pretend your judge is an editor and submit your cleanest, neatest, best work.

4. Put enough postage on your return envelopes. (As a contest coordinator, I once spent a few dollars of my own money to add postage to under-stamped entries I needed to return.)

Got all that? Good. Now, get going and send in your entry.

The deadline's coming faster than you think.

CHAPTER 23

Contests, Schmontests

by Rebecca Wade

CONTESTS. My favorite nerve-wrecker. A nice boost when used correctly. A stinging slap in the face when they aren't, and you let low scores derail your dreams. As far as I can tell, there are only two reasons for entering contests. One, to receive feedback. Two, to catch the eye of an editor.

There are a few contests that offer valuable critiques. The judges are selected carefully, and in some cases, you are guaranteed a certain number of published opinions. If your aim is to receive a fresh eye, then these contests can be wonderful.

Other contests offer no feedback whatsoever other than an unexplained score on an itsy-bitsy line. These are useful only if you score high and win the attention of an editor. Let's face it. In these contests, we're taking a gamble as surely as if we moseyed up to the edge of a blackjack table and slapped down our $25 entry fee. The dealer, dealing our manuscripts out to crabby or happy judges, can beat us any and every time. Sure, you can hedge your bet with a high-quality hand. But the dealer still holds the advantage; the numbers are against you.

Many of us enter the Golden Heart. Being the good gambler that I am, last year I hedged my bet—by entering two manuscripts. Then, on

April Fools Day (the day the finalists are announced), I held my breath every time the phone rang. For one incoming call, I vividly remember how my caller ID displayed "out of state call" on its mini-monitor. Heart pattering wildly, I picked up the phone, sure one or both of my babies had snuck into the finals.

"Hello?" I said, employing my most gracious and humble voice.

"Mrs. Wade . . . " a cheery voice said, "this is Jerry with American Express. And I'd like to tell you about an exciting new financial program we're offering our members. Blahbety blah blah blahhhh . . . "

Hope! Disappointment. *Hope!* Disappointment.

Needless to say, I didn't get the call. It was a tough day. The thing about my suffering on April 1 is this. I knew the contest would be tough to win. I understood that it was a roll of the dice. And I didn't gnash my teeth and shake my fist when I didn't make the finals, because for me, the potential reward inherent in the Golden Heart is worth the long odds every year.

Not long after, I got my scores back. My marks ranged from 8s all the way down to a 4. Eight meant "nearly flawless." Four meant "below average." I'll tell you frankly that I drop-kicked that four. Shrugged, then sent it spiraling into outer space. I hope it's still going.

Some believe contests are good for recognition, kudos, or back pats. Personally, if I'm not going to get worthwhile feedback and if my work is never going to pass under the eyes of an editor—then I don't enter. There are a lot less expensive ways to be encouraged in this business.

This is the cardinal rule of contests: use them, but don't let *them* use *you*. You can enter contests for the enjoyment of the gamble, for the wild odds of the big win, or for the good advice the judges might offer. If you lose, smile and shrug and drop-kick those low scores that threaten to shove your confidence and joy off-course.

Say "Contests Shmontests" until your tongue ties.

But never forget that it's ultimately the editor that matters most. Don't fall into the trap of substituting contest submissions for editor submissions. Because regardless of how your book fared in the latest contest, if it engages an editor so deeply that she can't stop reading . . . you'll end up holding a winning hand.

CHAPTER 24

Conferences
To Go or Not to Go

by Dovie Jacoby

THE ANSWER IS YES. Of course that's one woman's opinion, so I'd better come up with a good reason to spend up to a thousand dollars. And to lose days in which you could have written your bestseller. Okay, maybe fifty pages of your manuscript. Unedited.

Conferences are fun and inspiring. They are about learning your craft; networking with professional editors, agents, and publicists; and meeting people like you—other writers. They help you learn to have faith in yourself, and to gain respect for your craft of romance writing. They celebrate and support a writerly mix of hard work, talent, and a joy in storytelling.

For most aspiring novelists, the agent/editor appointments are first or close to first on their agenda. The business meetings are also important for some, although average members are content to let their chapter representatives attend these. If your representative has done his/her homework and hashed out views in your local RWA chapter, your views will be represented by proxy.

Conferences also offer great workshops. Topnotch speakers can give you just the right inspiring answer to improve your manuscript or solve your problem—or confirm what you've already accomplished in your work-in-progress. Or you might discover that the story you put aside awhile ago as not being saleable has now reached its time to go to market.

Any input and interaction with editors from the various publishing houses attending is invaluable. You may learn fresh, up-to-date insider information, perhaps that taboos once in place are gone or relaxed. You'll hear direct from the source what specific editors are looking for. (What do all editors want? A good, well-written story. Good writing is good writing, no matter the genre. That applies to category romance as well as single-title works.)

And then there's the fun.

The luncheons and dinners (which may or may not serve delicious food) always have wonderful speakers. Who could ever forget Anne Stuart's Greek Chorus or her boa? Or Theresa Madeira's story of a young soldier and his family, which caused everyone to shed tender-hearted tears? And there are speakers like Suzanne Brockmann who can light up the room with their energy, enthusiasm, and humor.

Here's a tip, however: the best source of information at conferences comes from the informal networking opportunities. Sitting in the bar or coffee shop with your friends can not only be lively and hilarious, but you can learn a lot if you listen. You'll hear stories of success, failure, and everything in between. You'll meet and make new friends. You'll hear that doing well in contests really does count with editors and agents—that they value the weeding and editing done for them by contest judges.

If national events aren't convenient or affordable, consider attending local chapter conferences. The fees are reasonable, the programs interesting, and there's usually an editor or agent attending (if the chapter's large enough), willing to talk one-on-one. It's an opportunity to get to know those editors, something that's not as easy to do in a large national conference with lots of writers vying for attention.

The best benefit of all, to my way of thinking, is what happens afterwards: you return home pumped full of renewed energy. You're ready to sit down at that computer to make writing history.

You know you can do it! Now, you're full of inspiration and know better just how to go about it. Conferences give you a big boost, and never fail to deliver plenty of what every writer needs: advice, support, fellowship, and a sense of how you and your talents fit in to the ever-changing world of romance writing and publishing.

CHAPTER 25

Preparing for an Appointment with an Editor or Agent

WHENEVER I'VE WORKED THE DESK at writers' conferences for appointments with editors and agents, I've often seen writers waiting in line, clutching their note cards with white knuckled hands. They tremble. They sweat. They tend to babble a bit, too. It always made me want to hug them and say, "There, there."

Because, really, editor and agent appointments are not that scary. Despite what you may have heard, editors and agents are ordinary human beings, just like you or me! If an editor or agent weren't looking for new talent, they wouldn't be there. So relax. The fate of your career does not entirely rest on this face-to-face meeting.

But, with preparation and confidence, this face-to-face meeting could be the beginning of good things for your career. Personally, I've done many pitches to agents and editors at these appointments.

Every time, I've walked away with a request for a submission. I've never had a pitch shot down.

What's my secret?

Preparation and confidence.

Preparation

Let's talk about getting prepared. First, new writers should realize that you need to be ready with a completed manuscript. If sufficient interest is shown in your pitch, be prepared to send that editor your work immediately, marked "per your request" or "requested materials."

Usually, editors, if interested in your work, will ask you to mail your novel to their office. They don't want to lug home a suitcase full of manuscripts.

While famous writers can pitch a story via a proposal only, and get it reviewed based on the idea and their track record, you need to have your story finished.

So before you make that appointment, make sure you have a complete manuscript—and synopsis—finished and in good shape for submission. If you don't, then wait until you do.

But let's say you're ready, and you've made your first appointment. Now what?

Well, for starters, when was the last time you read through your story? If it's been a while, then I suggest that you give it a reading a few days before your appointment. It's amazing the number of pertinent details you can forget over time about your own work. Get back in touch with your story by giving it a thorough review.

Next, read your synopsis aloud. If you can, tape yourself reading. The idea is to get accustomed to talking comfortably about the characters and plot of your story. Then, listen to the tape. Are your descriptions clear? If not, then rework your synopsis to clarify any fuzzy parts.

Now let's work on your pitch. Can you summarize your story in one or two sentences? For new writers, this might sound impossible. You need to be able to do this, though. A one-sentence summary gives you the perfect launching pad for your story pitch. From there, you can expand in whatever direction the editor or agent wants to go.

Example: *Two lovers meet in dreams across space and time to change the fate of the universe.*

This is a one-sentence summary for a three-book futuristic series. By starting with this summarized version, all in one sentence, I can then anticipate the editor or agent's questions. *How* do they meet in dreams? *How* do they change the fate of the universe?

By anticipating possible questions, I can be prepared to answer them confidently. So after creating your one-sentence pitch, consider the questions you might be asked. Write them down on paper. Then practice the answers. Better yet, go back to your tape recorder, read the likely questions, and give your answers aloud.

A word about note cards. My advice: ditch 'em. Okay, they make a nice security blanket. But if you are truly prepared for your meeting, you don't need your blanky, do you? Besides, if you are busy looking at your cards, how can you also look the editor or agent in the eye? How can you tell if you are capturing their interest?

If you truly feel you must have something to hold on to, then write your one-sentence pitch on a single card. As for the rest (your characters, setting, and plot), you should know everything there is to know. Fumbling through your cards for a description of your heroine doesn't make the best impression. Ditch the cards and have confidence in your ability to describe the story.

Feel better prepared now? If you done all this, you're ready to pitch your story.

Confidence

So, you walk into the appointment room. And there he or she sits . . . the editor or agent who "holds the fate of your career in their hands."

Wait a minute! If you go into the interview with this kind of attitude, then of course you're going to be scared. Before you walk in that room, let's get your head on straight.

The person in that other chair is an editor or an agent. Period. You likely will have to go through this process many times before selling a book (although you might be a Cinderella girl and sell one on your first try). Whichever fate is in store for you, this meeting is merely one more step on your path to publication.

You've already taken the most important ones. You started a book. And you finished it. That's something only 25% of new writers ever do. That's makes you special—and naturally of some interest to this agent or editor. Have confidence in your accomplishment.

So take a deep breath. Let it out slowly. Then walk in, hold out your hand, and introduce yourself.

From my first experiences doing this, I discovered there was often an awkward moment, as I sat down and waited for the editor or agent's first question. My trick for smoothing that one over: ask the first question. Smile warmly and offer something like: "Would you like to discuss my writing credentials first, or should I simply tell you about my story?"

By taking the initiative and asking the first question, I tend to feel more in control of how the interview will go. It boosts my confidence. I settle into the chair, look the editor or agent in the eye, and whichever option the person prefers, I know I can rattle off the answer. I can relax because I am prepared.

From there, simply follow the interviewer's lead. Answer every question as best as you can. Occasionally, they'll toss out something you didn't anticipate. Should that happen, take the time to think before you answer.

Most editor and agent appointments typically last between five and ten minutes. If you pitch your story well enough, you might find yourself granted a little extra time. The editor or agent might ask if you have other stories. If you do, go ahead and pitch them, too. Who knows? You might end up with submission requests for more than one piece of work.

You've probably noticed I haven't yet dealt with what to do if you're part of a group appointment. That's because I loathe them. No matter how small the group, there is always a Wanda Wannabe Writer who monopolizes more than her fair share of the group's time. By the time the appointment is over, most of the other writers would like nothing more than to punch dear Wanda in the mouth.

If a group appointment is your only option, then make yourself stand out—by being the writer most prepared to discuss her story *within her allotted time*. Look the interviewer in the eye and give her your one-sentence pitch. I'm willing to bet this will do far more to grab the editor or agent's attention than Wanda's endless prattling about how she got her story idea one day from her cat.

Because you, dear writer, have the edge over Wanda and her ilk. You showed up for your appointment feeling confident and were completely prepared.

Editors and agents like that. It's a sign of an author that can deliver the goods.

CHAPTER 26

A Community for Writers
Welcome to the RWA

THE ROMANCE WRITERS OF AMERICA is the largest genre writers group in the world. With over eight thousand members, it provides support and networking to its published and aspiring romance-writing members. The published authors of RWA write the novels that make up 55% of all popular paperback fiction sold, and are read by 41 million Americans.

RWA was founded in the sunny northwest-Houston borough of Klein in 1980. What began as the dream of five authors materialized to a petition of 68 founding members, and then swelled to become the 8,400-member strong association RWA is today.

"Romance Writers of America began as a dream in the minds and hearts of five published authors in a hotel room at the University of Houston's 1978 Southwest Writers Conference," says Rita Gallagher, one of the founding members.

Gallagher says the five founders first thought of forming a romance-writers association because they were frustrated with how little mainstream writing conferences had to offer them. "All of the workshops and visiting editors catered to poetry, nonfiction, or literature," Gallagher says. Although relatively small in 1978, the romance market was poised to explode into the $1 billion industry it is today.

By 1985, RWA had 4,000 members and was hosting its own comprehensive conference for the romance-writing industry. RWA made the confusing and intimidating world of New York publishing easy to understand and less formidable to unpublished writers. It educated published members about contracts, agents, packaging and promotion.

The fellowship RWA members enjoyed with other writers helped ease the isolation of a writer's life. It brought authors together to stand up for improved publishing practices. It also allowed them to pool their resources to promote the genre of romance fiction on a scale that publishers' budgets don't seem to allow.

Because the first RWA President—who worked tirelessly to launch RWA and see it prosper during its first years—lived in northwest Houston, the area was the natural site for the association's corporate office. Eventually, volunteer officers gave way to the hired professional staff that now facilitates the goals and programs outlined by RWA's elected Board of Directors.

Although RWA's corporate office is located in Texas, its members live throughout North America and the world. With 120 local RWA chapters in North America, romance writers everywhere have access to the camaraderie, advice, critiques, and support of fellow writers.

National Office

Romance Writers of America
16000 Stuebner Airline Dr.
Suite 140
Spring, TX 77379
Phone: 832-717-5200
Fax: 832-717-5201
Website: http://rwanational.org

Local & Regional Chapters

A complete list can be found on the RWA national website.

Special-Interest Chapters

In addition to its local chapters, RWA provides a variety of special-interest chapters that cater to the special needs of its members. The special-interest chapters were created to support RWA members who write in a particular subgenre. The chapters usually meet once per month through online discussions. Most offer an annual contest, a monthly e-newsletter, online resources, mentoring or critique programs, and a forum for discussion and encouragement.

To qualify for membership in a special-interest group, an applicant must be a current RWA member in good standing. There may be additional requirements for some chapters. Check online to see current membership dues or to download applications.

Special-Interest Chapters include:

Outreach International Romance Writers

www.oirw.org/about/index.html
"Provides support to members who live too far away to attend the functions of a regular chapter." Holds annual meeting each year at the RWA national conference. Benefits include *Outreacher* newsletter, annual contest, networking-by-mail program, and more.

The Beau Monde

www.thebeaumonde.com
Promotes romantic fiction, set primarily in the Regency period, 1811-1820 (dates can be extended). Members have online access to exclusive information, including The Regency Realm (online bibliography of 700+ historical references). Also offers online newsletter, *The Regency Reader*, free to anyone interested in Regency romances.

Faith, Hope, & Love (FHL)

www.faithhopelove-rwa.org
The inspirational special-interest chapter of RWA. Mission is to "promote excellence in romantic fiction, primarily inspirational romance." Members have access to *Herein Is Love* (bimonthly newsletter), markets, contests, e-mail workshops, database of critique partners, and a listserv where members can exchange ideas and industry information.

Futuristic, Fantasy, & Paranormal (FF&P)

www.romance-ffp.com

Promotes excellence in romance writing that has futuristic, science fiction, fantasy, time travel, or paranormal elements. Supports writers of this genre and provides current information through a newsletter, FF&P website, critique groups, and online discussion groups.

Mystery/Suspense (Kiss of Death)

www.rwamysterysuspense.org

Mission is "to promote and support the reading and writing of suspense and mystery fiction with strong romantic elements (woman's suspense, women-in-jeopardy, romantic suspense, and Gothic)." Benefits include a critique match-up service, *The Kiss of Death* bimonthly newsletter, online forums for networking and discussion, contests, and more.

Gothic Romance Writers, Inc. (GothRom)

www.gothrom.org

Provides a network of support, encouragement, and discussion for writers of stories with the elements of a true gothic romance: "heroine in peril, isolated setting, hero of questionable motives."

Published Authors Special Interest Chapter (PASIC)

www.pasic.net

Supports published romance authors. Offers a newsletter with industry information, NYC retreat with agents/editors, contests, networking, and support. Limited membership—authors must have at least one novel with a romantic theme published by a traditional publishing house; see website for details.

Electronic and Small Press Authors Network (ESPAN)

www.telltalepress.com/espan.html

New chapter devoted to promoting RWA authors who have published (or have a contract) with electronic or small presses. Members receive information on the industry, marketing, and the craft. Also strives to educate other RWA members, as well as the reading public, on the benefits of non-traditional publishing.

From the Heart Romance Writers

www.fthrw.com

Online chapter for RWA members who do not have access to a local chapter, but would like continuous contact with others interested in romance writing. Members have free access to online workshops, *Words From the Heart* monthly newsletter, critique groups, private e-mail discussion groups, scholarships, mentorship matching, and other benefits.

Hearts Through History Romance Writers

www.heartsthroughhistory.com

This group discusses different aspects of historical romance, and is open to published and unpublished historical romances.

RWA Online

www.rwaonlinechapter.org

Online chapter for RWA. Offers workshops, monthly programs, critique partners, plotting groups, online discussion/chat, and more.

Scriptscene

www.geocities.com/scriptscene2001

Offers scriptwriting information, tools, and support to help romance fiction writers write romance scripts and novels. Members also receive *The ReWrit* quarterly newsletter, e-mail list for access to archives/resources, and online access to movie scripts, e-mail support groups, and film industry information.

Writers of Non-Traditional Romance (WNTR)

Supports writers who employ different strategies or ideas for writing romance, using setting, characterization, conflict, and such in unique or "non-traditional" ways.

CHAPTER 27

Romance Novels are Love Stories

Interview with Charis Calhoon
Communications Director
Romance Writers of America

Rebecca Vinyard: What do you feel is the most common misconception about the romance genre?

Charis Calhoon: There are three myths that far too many people still associate with romance fiction. The myths are:

1. "These books" are all the same.

2. "These books" are all about sex.

3. "These books" are poorly written.

Here is why these "myths" are just that—and what romance fiction is really about.

1. These books are *not* all the same.

Romance novels are love stories. Think of how many couples you know—your parents, your colleagues, your friends. Everyone's life is populated almost entirely with couples, with people in pairs.

If you were to ask each and every couple that you know that age-old question, "So, how did you two get together?" each would have a different answer, unique to their circumstances. In short, there are as many different ways for two people to meet and fall in love as there are people in existence.

Romance novels are all love stories—yes. Romance novels all end happily—yes. But, just as in life, they are as diverse as the characters and situation crafted by their authors. Each one gives a distinct—and, because it is, after all, fiction—larger-than-life answer to the question, "How did you two get together?"

They are *not* all the same, no more "the same" than the personal love stories of every couple you've ever known to meet and fall in love. Falling in love is a singular experience. How, why, and to whom it happens is very unique. Each romance novels tells the unique story of two people falling in love.

2. These books are *not* all about sex.

Romance novels tell the story of the entire evolution of a couple falling in love and remaining there. Readers watch the couple when they first meet, when they first kiss, when they have their first fight, as they meet and overcome challenges, and, yes, when they make love.

However, no more time is spent in a romance novel on the love scenes, than on the dialogue scenes, or on scenes about the characters' childhoods, the first kiss of the characters, or their first quarrel.

For whatever reason, packagers and marketers have honed in on the one part of most romance novels that actually takes up a small percentage of the book: the love scene(s).

In actuality, however, romance novels are no more about sex than they are about meeting a soul mate; feeling acceptance for the first time; forgiving cruel parents; realizing a person does, indeed, have honor; or being unselfish for the first time.

3. These books are *not* poorly written.

Anyone who thinks romance novels are poorly written has not read Nora Roberts, Jennifer Crusie, Susan Wiggs, Anne Stuart, just to name a few—or any romance novel lately.

This is not your grandmother's romance novel. The only way to disprove this one is to encourage those who doubt it to study the subgenre of romance that may interest them . . . and get out there and give a current release a try.

Only the brightest authors are getting published today. And the books the romance genre has to offer can hold their own against any other genre fiction—against any other fiction.

Vinyard: How does your organization help romance writers during all the stages of their careers?

Calhoon: RWA's mission is to provide "networking and support" to published and aspiring romance authors. This is another way of saying we "help romance writers." Here are a few of the ways we do that:

The magazine

RWA publishes for its members a monthly 48-page magazine called *The Romance Writers Report*. It features articles on publishing, trends in the genre, essays about the romance-writing "life" or experience, and how-to pieces on the craft of writing.

A library of back articles from the magazine is available in the "members-only" area of RWA's website (www.rwanational.org).

The chapters

RWA has a network of 160 "local" chapters situated around North America, and online for members located in remote areas or outside of North America. Members who attend monthly local chapter meetings can hook up and coordinate with critique partners; hear guest speakers on the topics of publishing, researching, and writing; and generally socialize with other writers who are striving towards—or who have already achieved—goals in romance publishing.

The annual conference

RWA hosts a yearly national convention (in late July), which is attended by authors who are at every level of their careers—from *New York Times* superstar bestsellers to beginning writers.

Also in attendance are agents, editors, publicists, and publishers. The event allows authors to network with each other and with their publishers, and for new authors to pitch their work to acquiring editors. Also, authors and industry professionals teach more than 100 workshops at the conference on every aspect of writing, publishing, or the writing life.

The awards

RWA sponsors two major writing competitions each year. The RITA is for published members. This is for the best published romances in any given year, and is generally considered to be the highest award of distinction in romance.

The Golden Heart is for unpublished members. Winners (and often finalists) of this award usually sell their manuscript as a result.

The black-tie RITA and Golden Heart Awards Ceremony is the culminating event of each summer's RWA National Conference.

Advocacy & Promotions

RWA's Board also advocates on behalf of writers' rights to the publishing industry. Most recently, RWA's advocacy efforts affected a change to Harlequin Publishing's pseudonym policy, altering it in favor of authors.

Also, the communications department works to promote the genre and member authors. It helps introduce the genre to first-time readers, and encourages more voraciousness among current readers. The department targets its public relations and paid advertising to booksellers, the general public, distributors, librarians, and current and prospective romance readers.

Vinyard: Can contests help a writer improve their work?

Calhoon: RWA sponsors two national contests: the RITA for published novels and the Golden Heart for unpublished manuscripts. When writers enter their work in either contest, it is pitted against thousands of other books and manuscripts. The books and manuscripts that make the final round, or that win, certainly benefit from the distinction and promotion that goes to winners. However, the scoring for both contests is numerical; it isn't intended to give entrants detailed feedback on why their work did not advance.

However, most of RWA's 160 chapters sponsor their *own* writing contests. These smaller-scale contests often do provide written feedback from judges, with score sheets that read more like detailed critiques, and with comments on precisely what was good and what may need improvement.

For unpublished members, the entire contest process—regardless of which competition—helps prepare writers to submit their work to an agent or editor for publication. The routine of actually completing the manuscript by a given deadline, formatting it correctly, polishing it, and then sending it off is the same as formally submitting it to an agent or editor. When an unpublished author goes through the paces of entering a contest, he/she is generally ready to repeat the routine to an agent or editor.

Vinyard: How do conferences help writers improve?

Calhoon: The RWA National Conference provides education/learning opportunities for new and intermediate authors through more than 100 workshops on every aspect of writing and publishing.

For published authors, it's a fabulous opportunity to promote their work. Giving a workshop, participating in a book signing, meeting romance-fiction enthusiasts—all helps to direct new readers to their work.

For all attendees, networking opportunities abound. Whether writers are meeting agents and editors or other authors, everyone in attendance is interested in romance fiction. As a result, many business relationships are forged, friendships made, and general good feeling about the industry abounds.

Vinyard: What does the RWA do to promote romance?

Calhoon: Twice in the last four years, RWA has commissioned a romance-genre market-research study to tell us who is reading romance, where they live, their demographics, and the way they shop for books. We not only use this research to better tailor our own promotional efforts, but we also make it available to publishers, the media, and other interested parties. (To view the results of the study, click on the "Statistics" link at www.rwanational.org).

To booksellers and librarians, we distribute promotional pieces and hold a special "bookseller day" at our national conference to encourage them to realize the full potential of their romance section.

Romance fiction generates 55% of all mass-market paperback sales in America. We try to communicate to booksellers what a gold mine romance fiction can be, and offer tips on which books to push (our RITA winners), and how to make the most out of their romance aisle.

RWA also simply pushes the "three myths" message detailed above to journalists and academics interested in pop culture. We do our best to explain *why* the genre is so popular and why it sells so many books.

Section 4

Submitting Manuscripts for Publication

CHAPTER 28

Manuscript Formatting
A Survival Guide

I'VE READ MANY ARTICLES on manuscript formatting over the years. One thing they all had in common was the frequent use of the word "must." "You *must* use Courier." "You *must* mark extra line breaks with asterisks." "You *must* have 25 lines per page."

In my opinion, this absolute do-or-die attitude tends to frighten new writers. "What if I do it wrong?" they wail. "Will the editor send back my manuscript without even reading it?"

My answer? *Calm down.* Okay, there may be some editors fussy enough to reject a manuscript because the margin is under one and half inches. But you know what? I haven't found one yet. And whenever I do meet an editor, I often ask about this because I've wondered, what's the big deal about manuscript formats anyway?

True, there are certain instances, particularly contests, where formatting can be a big deal. Get it wrong and you can be disqualified. But the majority of the working editors I've asked about formatting have all said the same thing. They don't really care as long as the format is easy to read.

Think I'm kidding? Allow me to tell you the story of young Becky Vinyard, wannabe author, who submitted her first three manuscripts to her agent using the wrong font size. My agent never mentioned this formatting blunder until an editor, rejecting my third book, offhandedly remarked, "Tell her to use a 12-point font size. Ten is too hard to read."

Those first three manuscripts had been to dozens of houses, and although they were all marked with comments, none mentioned the font size. Number two had even gotten a request for a rewrite. But until book three visited that particular editor, nobody had said anything about their formats.

In fact, even the editor who mentioned I was using the wrong *size*, did not tell me that I should also quit using Times New Roman (which I happen to like) in favor of the more generally prescribed Courier. By the time I finally got around to reading about manuscript formatting (shortly after the above-mentioned episode, when I wondered what else I was doing wrong), I was just too attached to Times New Roman to switch. I still write and submit in Times . . . unless the guidelines of the publisher or contest specifically state they prefer Courier.

A couple of editors have told me they actually prefer Times. So the "You must use Courier" rule isn't all it's cracked up to be.

A better rule is: "Always check the publisher's guidelines first." This is essential not just because of formatting, but you need to know the desired word counts—and if the publisher is even looking for your kind of story in the first place.

So what else did I do wrong as a fledgling author? I italicized rather than underlined words I wanted to emphasize. And I didn't know I was supposed to have exactly 25 lines per page. (I'll be honest; I still ignore the lines-per-page rule . . . unless the specific guidelines say I need to be that exact.)

But despite the formatting faux-pas, I did get an agent, had numerous editors take the time to consider my work, and eventually got my work published.

So, what's the big deal? Well . . . what *is* a big deal is that you want your submission to look professional. So let's take it from the top and go over these rules. Perhaps once you know the reasons why they are in common usage, it will make more sense to follow them.

The basics

1. Use 20-lb. white paper. Slightly heavier paper (24-lb.) looks nice but doesn't affect its being read or not—and it costs more to mail. And use White. Not Pink or Scented Lavender or anything jazzy. White.

2. Use black ink. And a high quality printer. If your inkjet-produced pages look fuzzy—or, Lord forbid, you have a dot-matrix dinosaur of a printer—you'd be better off getting your manuscript run out at your local quick-print store. Just take them your diskette and ask them to print it out there.

   Why black ink on white paper, using a good printer? The high contrast makes the pages easier to read for the editor. (If you're not sure about the quality of your printer, have someone else read a few pages and see if they have any problems.)

3. Use paper clips or rubber bands to hold your pages together. Don't bind them! Editors prefer loose pages so they can easily have photocopies made for mark-ups or to circulate to other readers.

   When I package a submission, I usually put the cover letter on top. Then I put a paperclip on the synopsis. I either leave the body of the manuscript loose or use a big rubber band or two to hold it together.

4. Use those mailing envelopes with bubble-wrap inside to mail your manuscript. One of my small blunders of my early days was to use manuscript boxes instead of these envelopes. But the boxes are a pain for editors to haul around and take up too much space in their offices—while envelopes are lighter and stack better. They are also nearly indestructible. So save some postage; use the bubble-wrap lined envelopes.

Fonts

1. Twelve-point Courier is still considered the industry standard, although some authors prefer Times Roman or Arial instead. When in doubt, stick with Courier. In any case, use 12-point size for read-

ability. For my chapter heading and titles, I use 14-point. I use 10-point for page headers (see below), to set them apart visually.

2. Avoid colored fonts or fancy script. Do not use these. It just does not come across as professional.

3. Italics. For passages you want to be italicized in the finished book, the best practice is to underline them in your manuscript instead of italicizing them. Why? Because your publisher knows that underlining means "italicize me" in a manuscript. It dates back to the old days when books were typeset, and it was easier for the typesetter to see underlined words rather than italics. It's still the case. Underlining will make it much less likely that a key word to be italicized will be accidentally missed when your publisher converts your manuscript to a printed page.

Spacing

1. In general, single-space your query, cover letter, and synopsis. A few publisher and contest guidelines, however, do specify double-spacing for a synopsis. So, as always, check the guidelines first.

2. Double-space the body of your manuscript. And I like to allow a line space between the body and the header. Looks nicer that way.

3. Use 25 lines/page. To do this in Microsoft Word, go to the Format menu and select Paragraph. Under Line Spacing (where you typically indicate single or double), select the Exactly option and enter the number 25. There are other ways to do this, but I've rarely cared enough about about the lines/page rule to learn them all.

   Why is this useful? Because if you use this method, you can easily multiply the number of pages in your manuscript times 250 to get your word count.

   For years, this was the common practice because word processors weren't able to produce accurate word counts. But today, most word processors give you an instant, accurate word count—hence my apathy to the 25 lines/page rule. It is simply easier to use your word processor to count the words; then supply that number in your cover letter.

4. Extra line spaces are used when an author wants to indicate a transition to a new scene within a chapter. Simply hit the Return key twice.

   To emphasize a scene change, add a centered trio of asterisks or pound signs. (For no particular reason, I favor the pound signs.)

Cover letter

The cover letter should be the first page in your submission package. If an editor requested your manuscript either in answer to a query letter—or if the submission was requested via a face-to-face meeting—then say so. Also, write "REQUESTED MATERIAL" on the outside of your envelope (I usually use a black Sharpie for this) so your submission will go directly to the editor's desk.

If instead the publisher's guidelines indicate that submissions should consist of a synopsis and three chapters (this is not uncommon), then your cover letter, with those materials, act as a mini-query. Use it to tell the editor a little bit about the book and a little bit about you.

In any case, your cover letter should be concise! One page should do it. Use standard business letter format: single-spaced, starting with your contact information in the header, then the date (all this on the left side), followed by the editor's full address, then your salutation.

And for goodness sakes, *spell the editor's name right!*

Bio

I have always included a biographical page with my submissions. This includes a head-shot photograph, along with my education and writing credits. I don't think this is always necessary, but my agent got me into the habit. It can be useful if you have an interesting background and track record of writing.

Otherwise, for a first-time writer with no credits, it's best to leave this item out. Skip the bio, and let your writing do the talking instead.

Synopsis

Once again, I'm going to nag you: follow the publisher's guidelines. Synopsis format preferences vary widely from house to house. Some prefer double-spaced versions, others single-spaced. Some limit the number of pages your synopsis should run.

Know what they want *before* you submit.

On the synopsis, include your contact info and word-count total at the top of the page. Center your title and name. Include headers on all pages except the first.

Cover page

Not to be confused with a cover letter, a cover page basically serves as a title page for your manuscript. It presents your contact information, word-count total, and of course, your manuscript's title.

Your contact information (name, address, phone, and social security number) should appear in the upper left-hand corner. Word count goes in the upper right-hand corner. The title of your story is center page.

If you have an agent representing you, then only your name and social security number appear in the upper left-hand corner. The agent's contact information should be placed in the lower left-hand corner in place of your own. Got it?

A quick tip: save your cover page as a separate file from your manuscript. That way, it won't be included in your page count. For the same reason, also use separate files for your cover letter and synopsis.

First-page layout

The first page of every chapter should be set up differently from the rest of your manuscript. Drop down about a quarter of a page from the top. Center the chapter number and title, using a boldface if you choose. There should be no header on the first page. To do this in Microsoft Word, go to your Header/Footer format options and select Different First Page.

Headers

All other pages in the body of your manuscript should contain a header of some sort. I've seen these done in various ways. One option is to run it as a single, straight line across the top of the page. Another option is to group several lines in the right-hand corner.

Personally, I prefer the right-hand corner for my manuscript header and the straight line across the page for my synopsis. But use whatever you think looks best.

The header should contain:

- Book title

- Page number

- Author's last name

- Chapter number

I Wish Somebody Had Told Me...

1. Justification. Use "left-justification" (which creates a "ragged-right" edge on the right-hand side). Don't use "full justification." Don't worry about big, unused white spaces in your manuscript. The goal isn't to make it look like a book; it should look like what it is—a manuscript.

    Also, don't hyphenate if you cannot fit an entire whole word at the end of a line. Go to the next line (or let your computer do this, as it will if you are using left-justified only).

2. Dialogue. Put quotation marks around the speaker's words and, in general, punctuate inside the quotation marks.

    Examples:

    "I hate manuscript formatting," she said.

    Or:

    He said, "I hate manuscript formatting, too."

You might see exceptions to this in books or manuscripts that are published in the United Kingdom, where they use a different system that puts punctuation outside the quotation marks, like this:

"I hate manuscript formatting", she said.

But that's a British style difference, so don't punctuate that way for American publishers.

3. Endings. Don't put 'The End' or -30- or anything else at the end of your manuscript. When there's nothing left to read, the editor knows you're finished.

May I Have The Envelope Please?

Be sure to use a dark pen or marker to clearly label your envelope. Or type a label and stick it on.

Invest in priority shipping. Manuscripts tend to get mangled when they ship third-class.

Include a self-addressed, stamped envelope with your submission rather than loose return postage. It's far easier for an editor to lose stamps than an entire envelope. When you go to the post office, ask the postman to weigh your package with it open, and then have them apply the proper postage to your return envelope as well.

Tuck it inside, seal 'er up, and mail it in!

CHAPTER 29

Writing Query Letters
It's Not As Hard as You Think

THERE'S NOTHING AS MYSTIFYING to new writers as the query letter. New writers are often told, dauntingly, that the purpose of the query is to sell yourself and your story—all in one page or less.

"Huh?" Wanda Wannabe Writer might ask. "How am I supposed to sell my story in only one page? I can't even describe my book in one page! Help!"

Don't worry. Writing these letters is not as hard as you think. And a query letter's purpose is *not* really to sell yourself and your story.

A better way to think of it is as a letter of introduction. It doesn't sell a book directly; instead, an *intriguing* query is designed to generate interest. Once you grab an editor or agent's interest, then you have the chance to sell your book, at the next stage (the manuscript submission), via its merits.

So how do you write an intriguing query letter?

The Basics of a Query Letter

Let's start with the basics. Use a standard, single-spaced business letter format. Center your header and include your name, mailing address, phone number, and e-mail address. Centering your contact information makes it look somewhat like your letterhead. If you already have letter-head, you can use that instead, but make sure it includes these elements (especially your e-mail address, which is now how many editors prefer to respond if they are interested).

Then switch to left justification and put in the date. Skip a line, then write the editor or agent's title and address.

Skip another line, and begin with a standard business salutation, such as: Dear Ms. Editor:

Simple so far. Now for the tricky part: Summing up your book in one or two short paragraphs. Or better, summing up your book in one sentence. This sentence is called your "hook." It's the grabber that makes the editor sit up and say, "Wow! Cool concept!"

Impossible? Not really. Just use the *TV Guide* approach.

Check out this example:

> Melanie is a successful fashion designer who's engaged to the wealthy son of New York City's mayor. But love takes a detour when she goes back home to get a divorce from her estranged good ol' boy hubby and finds herself falling for him again.

This is my cable company's summary for the movie *Sweet Home Alabama*. It's only two sentences, but look at all the information you get.

- First you have the character descriptions. Melanie is a successful fashion designer, her fiancé is the wealthy son of NYC's mayor, and her hubby is a good ol' boy.

- Plus you have the plot. She goes home to get a divorce from the good ol' boy hubby and falls in love again.

- Third, and perhaps most important, this summary begs the reader to ask questions. Why did Melanie leave her good ol' boy hubby in the first place? Why did she get engaged to the rich guy when she was already married? What is she going to do now that she has fallen in love with her husband all over again?

Intriguing, isn't it? This is exactly what we're trying to accomplish in a query letter.

Notice this summary doesn't describe the *entire* story. There's just enough information to get you to consider ordering *Sweet Home Alabama* on pay-per-view.

Your objective is similar: to get the editor or agent interested in requesting your manuscript and synopsis.

And in you!

Introducing yourself

Which brings us to the second part of writing a query letter—introducing yourself.

If you have publishing credits, list them. If your education pertains to writing or the subject matter of your writing, mention it. List memberships in writing organizations or contests you have won.

In other words, this section is like a short resume. By listing your credentials, you prove you are qualified as a writer.

What if you *don't* have publishing credits or contest wins or belong to a writer's organization? Then keep the focus on your book.

And in all cases, close the letter with a simple thank you for the editor or agent's time.

Your query letter needn't be different for an editor or an agent. However, if you have a personal message to add—perhaps you met the agent at a conference—by all means mention it.

Just remember, a query letter is an introduction. To make a good first impression, keep the tone of your letter polite and professional.

Query Letter Do's and Dont's

- Do remember to include SASE with your query.

- Do use a standard font and plain white 20-lb. paper.

- Do keep the tone of your query professional.

- Do remember to spell the editor or agent's name correctly.

- Do check the agent or publisher's guidelines on the following:

  1. Is the agent or publisher open to submissions from new or un-agented authors?

  2. Does the agent or publisher accept simultaneous submissions? (Simultaneous refers to sending your query to more than one agent or publisher at the same time.)

  3. What kind of material is the agent or publisher seeking? There's no point in sending a paranormal romance to an agent or editor who's looking for historicals.

- Don't use cutesy fonts or fancy paper. (Trust me, this doesn't make a good impression on anyone in the business.)

- Don't compare your writing to a famous author's. (It will just lead to a "Yeah, right" response in the agent's or editor's mind.)

- Don't gush about how being a writer is your dream.

- Don't query if you are a new writer and your manuscript isn't finished.

- Don't demand a reply to your query right away. Instead, find out the editor or agent's average response time. If you don't get a response within that time frame (and I like to add two weeks to that, in case they're very busy), then write to ask if they received your query.

Sample Query Letter

Name
Address
Phone Number
E-mail Address

Date

Editor's Name
Editor's Title
Publisher
Publisher's Address

Dear Editor's Name,

I'd like to submit my manuscript, SINFUL RAIN, for your consideration. It's the story of a man who hires his ex-lover to find the family of the child he thought was his.

The private investigator, Justine Damaris, had her heart shattered [a few years earlier] when Reed Burkett told her their one-night affair was a mistake. Now he's back with the news that the child his scheming high-school sweetheart had claimed was his—isn't. To complicate matters more, the boy was not the sweetheart's child either. She died before telling Reed where she got the boy.

Justine would like nothing better than to throw Reed out of her New Orleans office, but Justine's father has disappeared and left her with all his debts—including the $75,000 he owes a loan shark. When Reed tells Justine to name her price, she sets the fee at $100,000. To her surprise, he readily agrees.

Reed would pay any price to win back Justine's heart. He knows he was wrong to let his fear of commitment stand in the way of their love. What neither of them counted on was that the price of love might be their lives.

I am a former e-zine editor and journalism major with two novels previously e-published. Also, I am a member of several writing organizations including the Dallas chapter of the Romance Writers of America.

SINFUL RAIN is a single-title romantic suspense story. I'd be happy to submit the synopsis and sample chapters or the completed manuscript for your consideration. Thank you for your time.

Sincerely,

Your Name

CHAPTER 30

Synopsis Basics

MANY WRITERS PUT SYNOPSIS WRITING in the same category as root canals. On occasion, it's necessary to get one done, but that doesn't mean you have to like it. At least with a root canal you can turn the problem over to the dentist. No such luck with a synopsis. It's up to you to get the job done.

This chapter covers "Synopsis Basics." The following chapter, "Anatomy of a Synopsis," looks at a real-life synopsis in depth, for a published book titled *Maggie's Wish*, courtesy of author Sharon Ihle. So you can actually practice what I'm going to preach.

So relax. We'll get through this together. Think of me as your friendly neighborhood dentist. So first, open wide . . . and we'll go over a quick check-up on the basic methods and then the individual elements of synopsis writing.

The TV Guide approach

I'm listing this first because it's *the* method of beginning a synopsis that's been extremely helpful to me. The idea is to take your story and sum it up in one or two sentences, just like *TV Guide* does for movies.

Consider this example:

> A story of star-crossed lovers aboard a doomed luxury liner as it
> moves towards its tragic destiny in the icy waters of the North Atlantic.

Everybody who recognized this as *Titanic* raise your hand. When you consider this is a four-hour movie, it's amazing the plot can be summed up in one sentence. And yet, all the major elements of story are here, aren't they?

Let's try another:

> Humiliated after discovering on a talk show her husband and best
> friend are having an affair, former prom queen Birdee Calvert packs her
> things, grabs her daughter and heads back to Texas. Distraught over her
> failed marriage she struggles to find her place in the world while trying
> to mend her broken heart.

Some of you recognized this as *Hope Floats*. (It wasn't as big at box-office as that boat movie, but I enjoyed *Hope Floats* more.) The point is that these two sentences nicely sum up *Hope Floats*. They provide setup ("humiliated on a talk show"), characterization ("former prom queen"), setting (Texas), and emotion ("distraught . . . she struggles . . . trying to mend her broken heart.")

So if the cable company can write a concise synopsis for such stories, we can too. Here's an example from my own work:

> Private investigator Justine Damaris is hired by her ex-lover, Reed
> Burkett, to find the family of the child he thought was his.

This is my one-sentence summary of a single-title romantic suspense novel I sold to Awe-Struck E-Books. It takes a 100,000+ word story and condenses it to one sentence.

A sentence summary like this is handy when I have to pitch a story in person. I can rattle off my one-liner and, hopefully, pique somebody's interest.

More importantly, it becomes the starting place for my synopsis. From this single sentence, I can expand out to whatever-sized synopsis

I need. And yes, I'm sorry to tell have to tell you this, but be prepared for your synopsis to come in several sizes. Some houses and contests only want a 2-3 page synopsis. Others may want five. Others don't set any limit—but the more detail you can pack into fewer pages, the better.

Always check the synopsis guidelines for any place you submit. In the long run, this will save you time and energy.

One last tip: you can also use the one-sentence approach to help summarize a scene or a chapter. Piece-by-piece, you can write summary sentences for each part of your story, then expand them until you have a full-fledged synopsis.

The Outline approach

I have a confession to make. I don't write the synopsis before I write the story.

Some of you might be nodding your heads. Others are probably shaking them in disbelief. Well, I do write a bare-bones outline, but I rarely follow it.

When I wrote my first synopsis, though, I did use the outline approach.

1. First, list all the *important* scenes in order.

2. Then, provide *characterization* for your major characters.

3. Finally, go back over it and add *emotion*. To make the synopsis more than just a dull summary, you need to explain how the various situations made your characters feel.

Be sure you've included all the major elements of your story. It should move ahead step-by-logical-step. If you want to establish background and setting, do it in your set-up. Don't get halfway through your synopsis and throw in a flashback reference. You'll lose clarity if you do.

We'll get into the individual elements of a synopsis in the next section.

Synopsis as proposal

Here's what author Sharon Ihle has to say about synopsis writing:

> Not too many of us love to write synopses. In fact, if my Larry comes home, hears me crying, and finds me ironing, the first thing out of his mouth is; "Writing a synopsis, huh?" Synopsis avoidance is the only thing that will make me pick up an iron.

See? Even experienced authors hate writing these dang things.

But most do recommend that you write your synopsis first. Most published authors sell a new work based on the proposal. As Sharon pointed out:

> This particular synopsis attracted a "new" publisher for me, and I hadn't written a word of the book. Sold [it] to a new publisher on that alone. A new writer won't do that as a rule, but if you can make your storyline simple and appealing, it'll sell the book.

Still, this doesn't mean you need to stick with the synopsis in every detail. As you read the synopsis example of Sharon Ihle's *Maggie's Wish* in the next chapter, you might notice the synopsis doesn't quite match the finished book.

This is because Sharon wrote the synopsis before she wrote the book. As she said:

> Even though I was muddled on what would happen when and where, the basic THEME of the story is there and that didn't change. I.e., 'Maggie hires Matt to find Rafe and bring him back to Holly for Christmas.' There's the underlying theme and no matter how I got there, that didn't change.
>
> It's important in a synopsis to find the focus of your story and make sure that it's very clear. The rest is basically unimportant.

So don't sweat over making your story match your synopsis or outline. You *don't* have to. You *do*, however, have to keep the basic theme in place.

As Sharon said, find your theme and make sure the focus of the story is clear.

The basic elements

1. The Set-up. This is the starting point of your story—its premise, location, time frame, and main characters' backgrounds. Just as you want to hook your readers with the first page of your book, you also want to hook the agent or editor with the first page of your synopsis.

    In Sharon Ihle's synopsis for *Maggie's Wish*, she accomplishes several of these elements in her first paragraph. The sooner you can establish your set-up, the better. Choose your words with care to get the background information presented in a concise *and* entertaining way.

2. Explanation of why. I'm listing this second, but this is something you should consider throughout your synopsis. If you pose a question, be sure to answer it. A synopsis is *not* the place to tease a reader; the agent or editor needs to know why something happens.

    For instance, say your story begins with the heroine quitting her job. You should explain *why* she quit.

    Reactions, decisions—whatever your character does within the framework of your synopsis, the reasons behind the actions must be clear.

    It wouldn't be enough to say, "Something happens to make the heroine change her mind." You must explain what that something is and *why* it made her change her mind. Clarity, clarity, clarity . . . make that your mantra as you're writing your synopsis.

3. Characterization. This is background, personality, occupation—everything that makes up your character. It is *not*, however, a physical description of your hero or heroine. Usually, the less said about their appearance, the better (unless the character's physical state affects her/him emotionally in some important way). For example: "She's extremely short and feels self-conscious about it."

Bear in mind that you want the reader of your synopsis to feel a connection with your characters. Focus on the emotional elements.

A deeply religious woman.
A savvy businesswoman.
An introverted professor.
An agitated accountant.

Phrases like these can be your friends; they give emotional and background information in just a few words.

Only name characters that play major roles in your story. Often, writers feel the need to mention secondary characters (maybe because they fall in love with them). But unless their actions affect the main plot throughout the story, don't include them—because if you do, you'll need to provide characterization and background for them as well. And this will inflate your synopsis! If a necessary reference to a minor character pops up only once or twice, you can simply say:

her best friend . . . his sister . . . etc.

4. Plot Points. These occur whenever your story departs from all that has gone before. Your character is forced to make a decision, or something unexpected and outside the experience of the character happens.

Do include *all* the major plot points in your synopsis. But do *not* include plot points for sub-plots. If it doesn't have anything to do with the main plot, forget it. Concentrate on theme always.

5. Conflict. A quick lesson in the two types of conflict: Internal conflict comes from within the character (e.g., she has poor self-esteem). External conflict comes from outside the character (e.g., a villain is blackmailing the hero).

To succeed in your synopsis writing, you need to present your conflict clearly. Which brings us back to the *why* element. *Why* is your heroine afraid of dogs? If she refuses to go to the hero's house because he has a Doberman named Rex lurking about, this is important information.

Or is your heroine refusing to go because she fears involvement—and she uses the dog as an excuse. If so, *why* does she fear involvement? And how does your hero feel about being rejected like this? Does he wonder if she rejecting Rex or him? Does rejection make him defensive because he seeks to be accepted? Does he resolve to never to have anything to do with her again?

Conflicts are the obstacles the main characters must overcome in order to achieve their goals. In a romance, the main goal is for the hero and heroine to fall in love and stay together. In a science fiction story, the goal might be to overthrow an evil corporation dominating the planet.

Whatever the goal, it can't be easy to achieve . . . otherwise there is no story. The readers need to know that there's a problem—and the *why* behind the problem.

6. Emotion. This element is of utmost concern for romance writers because for romance the magic is in the emotion. (Although I feel any synopsis of any novel in any genre should include it.) Embed emotion into your synopsis whenever you have the chance. Actions cause reactions. He kisses her . . . how does she feel about it? How does he feel?

   Emotion can make the difference between a dull summary of the facts to a lively recounting of your story.

7. Action. This drives most stories. It is probably the story element that will dominate your synopsis. In the synopsis, however, only include those actions that have consequences. If you heroine takes trip to the store for some eggs, don't include that unless something happens to her along the way. This is fairly obvious, I know.

   But as a contest judge, I've read many "synops" that included unnecessary action descriptions. If in doubt, leave it out.

8. Dialogue. There are two schools of thought here. Some folks say you should *never* include dialogue in a synopsis. Some feel a sprinkling of it here and there helps. My personal preference is the latter. If a specific line has more impact than a description of the same conversation, why not use it?

However, I wouldn't advise more than a few lines of dialogue. Don't go crazy and start quoting all over the place.

9. Black Moment. This is the moment when all is lost . . . when it appears your characters will never reach their goals. The odds are on the side of the opposing forces—and this is the moment when your characters realize it.

   In a romance, perhaps it's coming to a realization of conflict so overwhelming, it would appear that the hero and heroine will never be together. Whatever the genre, this moment of reckoning should not only be important to your story, but also to your attention-grabbing synopsis.

10. Climax. Your story has been thundering along, and everything that has gone before should lead up to this point. Whether it's the bad guy getting what's coming to him, the hero finally getting over his lack of self-esteem, or the heroine riding to the rescue, this is moment when it all happens. Naturally, this element should also be included in your synopsis, in a way that makes it clear: This is it!

11. Resolution. Here, all your loose ends get tied up. Any outstanding questions posed in your synopsis should be answered and resolved in a satisfying way. Yes, as we all know, the goal is for the hero and heroine to live happily ever after (or not, depending on your genre).

   Whatever the case, the synopsis needs to include the resolution to your story. This is not the time to play "guess the ending"!

Other essentials

1. Present Tense. The number-one essential: write your synopsis in present tense.

   Think of it as telling a friend about your book. Avoid passive word-usage. You want those words to flow evenly and keep the reader involved. Perhaps you've heard the saying that a writer's best work should be the query letter and synopsis. That kind of puts the pressure on, doesn't it?

I happen to believe a more accurate saying might be that a writer's *clearest* work should be the query letter and synopsis. Focus on the main story and avoid extraneous information.

2. Formatting. From my experience, most houses prefer double-spaced format, but some ask for single-spaced. As I mentioned earlier, *check the publisher's submission guidelines*. Or contest guidelines. (Am I making this point clearly enough?)

   The majority of submissions prefer that you give your contact information and word count on the upper left corner of the first page. On subsequent pages, include the title, your last name, and the page number in your headers.

3. Other Matters. For heaven's sake, make sure you spell the editor's name right. If you can't find it in the submission guidelines, a quick call to the editorial offices should get you that name.

   Always include an SASE with every submission. If you want confirmation that your submission has been received, a stamped, self-addressed postcard will do the job. If you want your work returned to you, make sure you affix the proper postage to an envelope large enough (and sturdy enough) to hold the material.

CHAPTER 31

Anatomy of a Synopsis
A Case Study

Based on MAGGIE'S WISH (a novel by Sharon Ihle)

I'VE ATTENDED MANY WORKSHOPS on this topic, probably, like many of you, in the desperate hope I'd learn enough to compose a coherent synopsis. Sometimes, a speaker will attempt to whip up the audience's enthusiasm by saying things like "Repeat after me . . . the synopsis is your *friend*."

With friends like these, I don't need enemies.

Okay, enough with that. Let's roll up our sleeves and get to work. Together, we'll be looking at Sharon Ihle's synopsis for *Maggie's Wish*.

The first part of a synopsis is the *Set-up*. Here's how Sharon's set-up begins:

> The sluggish days of summer are giving way to the crisper fall evenings of 1881 Prescott, Arizona Territory as Maggie Thorne glances out the kitchen window and sees her six-year-old daughter hoeing the pumpkin patch. Halloween is just two months away, which means that soon, Christmas will be upon them—again.

Sharon packs a lot of information in two simple sentences. In the first sentence, she establishes setting, a home in "1881 Prescott, Arizona Territory." She establishes the heroine, Maggie Thorne, and lets us know she has a six-year-old daughter. We discover the time of year, two months before Christmas.

She also gives us an inkling to Maggie's mood—anxiety over Christmas. We read on, because we wonder: *why* is Maggie worried about Christmas?

That's what your set-up should do. Establish location, character, and mood. But most of all, it should pique the reader's interest. Just as your novel should hook the reader on the first page, so should your synopsis hook the agent or editor.

Christina Dodd led one of the best workshops I've ever attended on synopsis writing. She said you should be able to get the initial set-up information across in one page or less. It's a good rule of thumb to work by.

To continue with Sharon's set-up:

> Just the mere thought of that most revered of holidays is enough to sink Maggie's spirits. Not that she has anything against Christmas itself. She has a lot to be thankful for when the sun rises each December 25. Her daughter Holly, whom she adores without reservation, came into the world at twenty minutes past eight on Christmas morning. A deeply religious woman, Maggie also thinks of the holiday as Christ's birthday, never failing to recognize it as such in a respectful manner.
>
> As the bread baker and pastry chef in a small restaurant owned by her Aunt Lorna, the holiday season also keeps Maggie happily productive and fills her coffers well enough to see her and Holly though the winter. But something supersedes all the good the holiday brings, a dark and dreary cloud that obscures the yuletide lights and dulls the sparkle in Maggie's wide brown eyes. Lord help her, how much longer can she go on this way?

Here Sharon establishes *Characterization*. We learn Maggie's occupation, that she is a spiritual person, and that she adores her daughter.

We also see that Maggie is more than just anxious about Christmas, she dreads it. We can feel her emotions and again we ask, why?

In the next section of her synopsis, Sharon tells us why by providing Maggie's background:

> She was a tall, plain-faced spinster of twenty-two with little hope of landing a man of her own the first time Maggie laid eyes on Rafe Hollister. At the time, a hard Utah winter had settled over the family farm, bringing with it the kind of cold that bites hollows in the chubbiest cheeks and freezes nose hairs stiff as pokers—and that was if a body stayed indoors. Rafe was close to dead the morning Maggie found him huddled in a corner of her father's barn.

> He'd been shot clean through the shoulder, and while the wound itself isn't life-threatening, the loss of blood made him pitifully weak. When Maggie comes across him, he's also nearly frozen clear through. She should have run and got her pa the minute she saw him lying there. She should have taken the gun from Rafe's stiff fingers and finished him off right there on the spot, saving them all a ton of grief.

> Maggie could have done a lot of things, anything but what she settled on once Rafe turned those big calf eyes on her and grinned that devil grin. If she had, she wouldn't be sitting at her kitchen table now wondering how in hell she was going to explain one more time why Santa Claus hadn't brought Holly the only thing she'd ever asked for; her very own daddy.

> It wasn't as if her first—and only—true love hadn't known the trouble Maggie was in. Spring thaw was late in coming that year. By the time Rafe had healed and Maggie had nursed him to his former robust self, she had a pretty good idea there would be a baby come winter.

> She told him, of course, sure he'd do right and take her away with him, but excuses why not spilled out of his mouth faster than the teardrops from her eyes. He was on the run from the law, a thing she'd pretty well guessed on her own, and although he hadn't done a blasted thing wrong according to him, he had to get it set right before he could settle down and raise a family.

Maggie can hardly remember flying into hysterics that day, but she recalls flinging enough of a fit over what her future held once her father got wind of her 'little' problem for Rafe to decide he ought to help her figure out what to do. After slapping her around a little, making damn sure she wouldn't alert her entire family to the fact that he was living in their barn, Rafe dipped into his overstuffed saddlebags, pulled out a wad of bills, and told Maggie to use the money to buy a train ticket. She chose the destination, Prescott, because her mother's sister lived there and would take her in until Rafe could join her.

On the morning Maggie runs away from home, Rafe tells her he loves her, shows her one more time exactly how much, and then promises to get square with the law and meet her in Prescott well before Christmas day. Six long years and six longer Christmases have gone by since then. And at each of the last four, a little red-haired girl cries fat teardrops all over her birthday cake at the close of that most celebrated day. This year, God willing, things will be different.

All the information Sharon includes here is important. We learn about Maggie's character and Rafe's. We see how they met and how they parted. We learn this relationship was the turning point in Maggie's life, causing her to move away from her home in Utah to Arizona.

Most importantly we now know *why* Maggie dreads Christmas: because it is also her daughter's birthday—and her daughter wishes for her daddy to come home every year.

This ends the *Set-up* and brings us to the first *Plot Point*.

This year, Maggie has hired a retired Texas Ranger, a man just a few years older than she who has given up the badge and hard chases because of a bum leg. Her friend, the sheriff of Prescott, is also a friend of the ranger, a man he believes is perfect for the job because he's very, very good at tracking people who don't know they need tracking. People like Rafe Hollister who have lost their way.

Plot Point: Maggie has decided to do something about her daughter's unhappiness. It is the departure from all that has gone before.

We understand her motivation for doing this because of the background information Sharon provided. It is also our first introduction to the hero. We know that he's a good tracker. In the next paragraph, Sharon tells us about Maggie's reaction to him—and also sets up the *Conflict* between them.

> Once she meets Ranger Matt Weston, Maggie is suddenly at a loss to explain her circumstances and finds herself making up excuses for Rafe, not just for Holly's sake, but also for her own. After all, she'd once loved Rafe enough to bear him a child born in shame—how could she show herself as a woman who'd allowed that love to die? Wouldn't that make her time of sinning with Rafe somehow more depraved?
>
> Matt Weston would definitely think so—Maggie senses that in the man after one look in his silvery, no-nonsense eyes. For reasons she can't imagine, this near-stranger's opinion of her is extremely important. Evading the truth rather than lying to Matt, Maggie simply explains that her man ran out on his responsibilities and that she wants him brought back to her—alive and well. She believes that explanation will give the former lawman the impression that Rafe is her husband, and why shouldn't it? Her Prescott neighbors have long believed the very same thing.

Maggie doesn't tell the whole truth about her relationship with Rafe because she's afraid that if Matt knows she's an unwed mother, he won't help her.

And because, to her, *his* opinion of her is extremely important. We can already sense she is attracted to him. We understand her motivation and why she chooses not to reveal the truth.

In the next paragraph, we are introduced to Matt's character from his point of view. You might call this the *Second Set-up*. We get Matt's background and his current motivation.

At thirty-two years of age, Matt Weston hates his early retirement with a passion, and for what he sees as two good reasons: The first, and hardest to take, is his exclusion from the manhunts, the feel of his own blood thundering in his veins as he runs his quarry down. The second, and somehow more threatening than a cornered outlaw with blazing guns, is his sudden vulnerability to the single ladies in town.

For over thirty years Matt has easily avoided the perils, and he has to admit, the responsibilities of turning his life over to a member of the fairer sex. Now that he is almost desk-bound, he's practically tripping over available women, and even more alarming, rapidly running out of excuses for remaining a bachelor.

Here we learn he's a man of action, forced into retirement. We also know that he is not looking for a woman, that he prefers the bachelor life . . . until . . .

Funny how that final excuse—not to mention a man's mind—can vanish with the blink of a warm brown eye. A pair of them, to be exact, each rimmed by a lush bank of lashes the color of pitch. He has no business looking into those eyes or thinking thoughts that don't include ways of catching up to Maggie's wandering husband, but Matt can't seem to stop himself. He is an honorable, professional man, one who never lets his personal life get in the way of business, so why in hell can't he keep his mind on his work whenever she is around?

He supposes his lapse of ethics has something to do with Maggie's gentle ways and honest charms, the kind of beauty that fairly radiates the goodness in her heart. Not that he believes any of those things can excuse his utter fascination with the lady. He has a job to do, and sets out to do it with an almost personal vengeance.

Here we have Matt's initial *Conflict*. He's determined to do his job, but his attraction to Maggie is getting in the way. Since he is an honorable man, he's disgusted with himself for having feelings for the "married" Maggie.

In the next section, we leave the Second Set-up and begin the *Action* of the story.

> It doesn't take Matt but two weeks to locate the bastard—the precise opinion he forms of Rafe Hollister within minutes of locating the man.
>
> The meeting takes place at a rundown saloon in El Paso when Matt stumbles over a drunken Rafe who is passed out on the floor. When Rafe finally comes to, Matt decides that Miss Maggie is in for a rude shock—and Miss Maggie is the way Matt thinks of her no matter how hard she hints that she's actually married to this stinking outlaw.
>
> While Rafe is still unconscious, Matt takes him into his custody and discovers that he has been wounded—most of his left ear is blown to smithereens and a bullet fragment is lodged in his right wrist. Although Matt wishes whoever wounded the man had been a better shot, he tends to the injuries Miss Maggie's 'lost' husband has suffered, then binds him hand and foot and tosses him in the back of his wagon.

Again, we are shown Matt's conflict. He can't bear to think of Maggie as a married woman. His feelings for her affect his dealings with Rafe.

He always keeps Maggie's best interests in mind. *Emotion* is the most important element in a romance synopsis. You should convey what the characters are feeling as often as possible. A synopsis is *not* a summation of the story's action. If you just do that, you aren't doing enough.

> When Rafe sobers up and awakens to find himself traveling west toward Arizona Territory, Matt informs the miserable bastard that his wife and child are looking for him, and that he's been hired to take him to Prescott. Far from being grateful, Rafe begins cursing Maggie, calling her a horse-faced spinster among other things and declaring that she was lucky to have gotten as much as she did from him—a good time and the only piece of 'loving' she'd ever get from a sane man. He tries to go on raving about Maggie, assuring his captor that he wouldn't have touched her at all had he not been weak and crazy in the head from loss of blood.

Here we are introduced to the secondary character of Rafe. As a rule, the fewer secondary characters that appear in a synopsis, the better. The exception is if they are essential to the story, as Rafe is in this one.

For example, back at the *First Plot Point* paragraph where Sharon mentioned Maggie and Matt's mutual friend, the Sheriff of Prescott, we aren't given his name or background. Why? Because his only function is to get Maggie in touch with Matt.

Rafe, on the other hand, is an important character. We want to know *why* this man would abandon his "wife" and child.

> When the ranger pulls the wagon to a halt and climbs down from the driver's seat, Rafe is certain he is about to be set free. Instead he receives the worst beating of his miserable life. When he comes to, Rafe quickly discovers that both of his eyes are swollen shut, his lips are split and caked with blood, and he is hanging by his wrists, including the injured one, from a rafter inside a darkened barn. Then, through what is left of his ear, he hears the voice of the former ranger as he explains the terms of Rafe's "pardon."

This section brings us to the *Second Plot Point*. Matt has decided to depart from the simple plan of bringing Rafe to Prescott. He now wants to reform him for Maggie's sake.

Plot points are *turning points* in the story. Here is Matt's first turning point. He gives Rafe an ultimatum. And Rafe, seeing little choice, agrees to be reformed.

> You will submit yourself to a month of intensive training as a decent law-biding citizen and loving husband and father, he is told. This will take place in Prescott where Miss Maggie Thorne can follow your progress and make a final decision about whether she should or should not accept your marriage proposal—and yes, you will ask her to be your wife. You will then abide by Maggie's decision and do your level best to uphold it for the rest of your natural life.
>
> If you chose not to do those few things, Matt informs Rafe, there's another option for you to consider: You can continue to hang by the

wrists here in this abandoned barn which happens to be situated on the Mexican side of the Rio Grande. This will undoubtedly bring your life to a very unnatural end.

Rafe quickly accepts the original terms and keeps his complaints to himself during the rest of the journey to Prescott. Once they settle into Matt's cabin, Rafe is shackled to a chain hanging from an overhead beam, but otherwise free to move about the perimeters of the room.

He also proves to be a surprisingly apt pupil, learning how to speak and behave like a gentleman in just a few weeks, and actually asks to see Maggie again in the hopes of meeting his young daughter.

Now, we see the consequences of that last decision, from Matt's point of view:

For Matt, it is a time of raging conflict. Although he works hard to turn the outlaw into someone worthy of Maggie and Holly, from the basest part of his soul, Matt is praying that Rafe will fail. His visits to Maggie each day to report on Rafe's progress are taking a toll on his sanity, not to mention his body. He awakes in a sweat night after night, his dreams filled with images of the woman he has fallen in love with. Even worse, he has convinced himself that he sees his own frustrations and needs each time he looks into her expressive eyes.

This paragraph describes the emotional consequences of Matt's decision because we are able to see the internal conflict he is suffering. For every decision you describe in a synopsis, you should also show the consequence, not only in the action, but also in the *emotion*.

Notice the words used here to convey emotion: raging, basest, frustration. All are emotion-rich words. New writers will often leave this element out of their synopsis—how the action makes the characters *feel*.

It is as Thanksgiving draws near that Matt slips into the darkened coffee shop late one night to discuss Rafe's progress, and finds Maggie awash in tears. He takes her in his arms, comforting her, and asks her what is wrong. There is no way she can explain how much her feelings for Matt have grown or to let him know how badly she wants him—not after he's been working so hard to make her "almost" husband presentable enough for her to marry. Even Maggie can't understand how she can have such deep feelings for Matt when the man she thought she wanted is just up the street. In spite of her less-than high opinion of her lustful nature, Maggie's desire for Matt continues to build, turning her tears into sobs.

When Matt's attempts to comfort her become passionate, Maggie does nothing to cool his ardor, allowing herself instead to linger over his forbidden touch. Unable to deny herself the man she so desperately yearns for, Maggie succumbs to temptation.

Hallelujah, we're at the *Third Plot Point*. (I say hallelujah, because I always enjoy the part of the story where the heroine and hero succumb to temptation.) Here Maggie and Matt allow their feelings for each other to reach the physical level.

It is another turning point, an *emotional* turning point, and as such, will have consequences. These are described in the next paragraph of the synopsis.

Cause and effect, folks. Show the reaction to every action. (Am I stressing this enough?)

Although he wouldn't trade the night spent with Maggie for his own life, Matt is plagued with guilt and self-loathing the next day, taking the entire blame for what happened between them upon himself. He avoids Maggie as best he can while continuing to encourage perfection in this less than perfect clump of humanity known as Rafe Hollister, but it isn't easy. He punishes himself with thoughts of turning Maggie's perfect husband over to her once his job is done, and polishes the outlaw to perfection if for no other reason than just to see her smile, to witness for himself a sparkle of happiness in those sad brown eyes.

Poor Matt. Being the honorable man he is, he blames himself for what happened. His guilt leads him to avoid Maggie . . . and to work harder on making Rafe a better man for her. This is the consequence of their succumbing to temptation.

> On December 15 and according to plan, Matt arranges the long-awaited reunion between Maggie and Rafe. She feels awkward in Matt's presence, certain that the coolness he exhibits toward her is due to her immoral behavior, but remains composed as he leads her into his cabin to visit her lost love.
>
> Although it's been almost seven years, Maggie notices immediately that Rafe still has those calf eyes and a devilish grin to match them. When he turns those considerable charms on her, for a fleeting moment Maggie becomes that lonely, vulnerable farm girl again, grateful and smitten by what she'd once mistaken as true love.

And as we see, their tryst also had consequences for Maggie. She feels guilt over her behavior. But, this doesn't stop her from being vulnerable to Rafe's charm on their first meeting either.

> Witnessing Maggie's rebirth, glimpsing the sweet hot luminance in her painfully honest eyes is more than Matt can tolerate. Without a word, he takes his broken heart and slips out of the room, leaving the pair of lovers with the only thing he has left to offer them—their privacy.

My heart just aches for Matt. Doesn't yours? Again, as another consequence of his actions, he made Rafe into the perfect man. Now he has to live with how Rafe makes Maggie feel.

Notice the emotional level of this simple paragraph. It has action, but it also makes the reader feel Matt's pain. This is Matt's *Black Moment*. The Black Moment, you'll recall, is when the character realizes he will not achieve his goal.

Of course, Maggie is nobody's fool. She immediately gets hold of her emotions and for nine days, grills Rafe about his intentions.

The click of the latch snaps Maggie out of yesterday and brings her back to the independent, self-reliant woman she is today, but by then, Matt is gone. Feeling in control of herself again, and of Rafe for the first time ever, she sits him down, chews him up one side and down the other for his sins of the past, then queries him about his plans for the future. Where and how, she wants to know, will those plans affect Holly? What kind of a father does he expect to be and how long will he be there for her physically, emotionally, and financially? Exactly what does he expect in return?

This interrogation continues for nine days with Matt outside the door of the cabin listening in. No matter how far Maggie corners Rafe or how tough the questions, he always comes up smelling like a rose. All he wants out of this life, he swears, is to have Maggie as his wife and to be a father to his daughter at long last.

Throughout this period, Matt continues to instruct Rafe on the ways of gentlemen (even though he hasn't behaved like one himself), fulfilling the task he was hired to do. When Christmas morning finally arrives, Maggie pleads with Matt to visit her home at sunup and share in the spoils of a job well done. Although he is reluctant, his heart heavy, the ex-lawman arrives just moments before Rafe does.

Then Christmas day arrives, and we have the *Climax* of the story.

As Maggie carefully positions her former lover near the Christmas tree, then calls Holly to come downstairs and see what Santa has left for her, Matt can barely watch when the sleepy-eyed youngster drags into the room. Once she sees a stranger by the tree, and that stranger identifies himself as her father, Holly lets out a strangled cry and vaults into his arms. In moments the rest of them—Maggie, Matt, and even Rafe— are awash in tears.

This is the *Climax*, the moment Sharon has been building towards since the first paragraph of the synopsis: A happy Christmas morning.

After the *Climax* . . . comes the *Resolution*.

Giving her daughter a few minutes alone with her father, not to mention, time to pull herself together, Maggie tugs Matt into the kitchen and closes the door behind them. Remarking that she ought to be celebrating with the joyous pair under the tree, Matt thanks her for inviting him, then heads for the door, intending to let the newly reunited family enjoy their holiday in private. Maggie softly asks him to stay, even through Christmas dinner if he likes, but Matt can't understand why she'd want a used-up lawman hanging around on Christmas day, especially since his job is done. Maggie gently kisses Matt's weathered cheek and thanks him again for making Holly's wish come true.

She then thanks him for the changes he made in Rafe Hollister, in particular the way Matt convinced Rafe to humble himself by begging her to marry him during each of the past nine days. It's done her heart good, she confesses, and also freed her enough to realize that she doesn't love Rafe and probably never did.

Her answer for the past nine days, she says, has been an unequivocal, no, thanks to Matt Weston. With that, Maggie again kisses the man she really loves, this time square on the mouth.

Overwhelmed by her confession, unable to keep from touching her a minute longer, Matt takes Maggie into his arms, then asks her what she would do if he were to have an unfulfilled wish the way Holly did. Who could I hire to help me make my wish come true? he wonders aloud.

The Resolution: Maggie's actions and emotions are resolved when she realizes Matt is the man she always wanted, not Rafe. This also resolves Matt's conflict, when he realizes he is now free to love Maggie.

This moment carries the most emotion, and Sharon emphasizes this by using dialogue in the next two paragraphs.

Maggie swears if there's anything she can do to help, she'll do it. Anything. Vowing to hold her to that promise, Matt pulls her even tighter into his embrace and whispers, "See if you can help me with this—I wish I could find a beautiful woman to marry who has laughing brown

eyes, kissable lips, and is tall enough for me to kiss back without bend-
ing myself in half."

As tears of joy roll down Maggie's cheeks, Matt loosens her hair from
the coil at her neck and fans it between his fingers. "Make sure the lady
also has golden brown hair that smells of cinnamon and apples, and that
she loves me at least half as much as I love her. When you find her, make
sure to tell her that I promise to make her wishes come true for the rest
of her life."

The dialogue and the action precisely describe this emotional moment.
Some folks say never use dialogue in a synopsis, but I'm all for it when
it can convey the feeling better than a summary.

And so as Christmas of 1881 comes to a close, a daughter's wish for
her very own father is fulfilled; an outlaw who thought he never wanted
fatherhood or to know the true miracle of Christmas, finds both along
with more joy than he's ever known; and a man and a woman find
themselves free to love one another with everything they have to give,
joining together as one to wish for a lifetime of happiness together.

This is a great final paragraph. It ties everything together by describing
the changes to each of the main characters lives.

This is a wonderful example of a synopsis. It carefully covers all the
bases, pulls you along into its conflicts and consequences, its themes and
resolutions. It delivers a sense of a passionate, emotional story—one that
readers will want to read . . . and that editors will want to buy.

Writing a synopsis is not that hard. Just remember it's more than just
saying what happens. The synopsis must tell *why* and reveal how the
characters feel and react to the events that happen to them.

CHAPTER 32

Bagging The Right Agent

by Rosalyn Alsobrook

U NEARTHING A GOOD AGENT is hard enough, but locating the *right* agent can be downright nerve-racking. Once you have decided you need an agent (or if things are not quite working out elsewhere and you need a *new* agent), how do you go about finding the best one to represent your work?

This is not an easy question to answer.

Moving on from a current agent

If you have an agent you are not happy with, the first step is to review his or her services. What proposals do you have out there submitted under that agent's name? Does he or she agree that the partnership isn't working, and is he or she willing to relinquish those represented works to a new agent, either immediately or after a transition period?

Check the terms of your contract. It should specify a process for ending the relationship, including what happens with specific works and submissions currently under consideration at publishing houses.

Find out if you have to wait until all submissions have been rejected and are no longer under consideration by anyone else. More likely there is a specified time period (anywhere from 30 days to 6 months), after you give notification that you intend to end the relationship, in which the old agent has one last chance to submit and sell your work before you go elsewhere with it.

Keep in mind that if one of your works under consideration in the transition period is accepted for publication, your old agent will still be the person to negotiate that sale, and will then have earned his or her percentage as the "agent of record." It's legal, and it's fair.

In the event that your contract does not specify the process for transferring your current and future work to a new agency, you might request a written release for specific titles.

Preparing to find a new agent

But suppose you are already free and clear of your first agent, or you have not had your work represented yet? What's the first step?

If you're like me, the first thing you need to do is get the butterflies out of your stomach. There is nothing to be afraid of. Contrary to rumor, agents are more human than barracuda.

The second thing to do is ask around. Talk with other writers at conferences or on electronic bulletin boards. Find out who likes which agents and why. If their reasons make sense to you—if these agents have traits you'd like to see in your own agent—then write down that agent's name.

Compile a list of at least four names that interest you. Next, make sure you have the current address and telephone number for each. I advise calling, rather than writing a letter, because it moves the process along more quickly. I suggest that you set aside enough time to talk to each agent on the same day (should you be lucky enough to catch them all in their offices). If you can hit them all within the same day, it will be easier to compare their services.

Making the calls

In no particular order, call and ask to speak to the agent. If someone else answers and asks who is calling, give your name and state that you are calling to ask a few questions of the agent as a potential client. Don't give this other person your whole spiel; save it for the agent. Same goes for an answering machine or voice mail. State who you are and why you're calling, but don't go into depth.

When the agent comes on the line, speak with confidence, but don't be overbearing. State again who you are, that you are researching different agents for representation, and that you would like to know a little something about how he/she does business.

Have your important questions ready, in front of you, in written form. But don't read them off like a drill sergeant. Work questions into the conversation as you go, letting the conversation take a life of its own. This will allow you to find out if you would be compatible with this agent. It also allows for a drift that can be just as informative, if not more so, than the items you have on your list.

After discussing how he/she does business and asking for the names of a few references, it's time to talk about you. Have another list ready: what you've written, what you've published (or what contests you have won), what you are currently working on, what you plan to work on next, and which editors hold submissions at the moment.

If you are in the transition stage of leaving your first agent, be sure to mention that. You don't have to give his/her name if you don't want to, but the new agent you query should know that you've had previous representation.

Ending the conversation

After that, if the agent is still interested and hasn't indicated he/she is ready to end the conversation, then just chat for a few minutes. Find out what types of writing he/she likes (or does not like). Get to know each other on a more personal level. Go with the flow.

But whatever you do, don't commit.

This is what I call the "Alsobrook Rule." Even if you really like talking to this person and like what they have to say, *don't commit* during that first telephone call. Wait until you've had more time to think about it. There is still a chance the next agent might impress you more.

Do, however, promise to send some material if they ask to see it.

Evaluating the responses

As soon as you hang up with the agent, make written notes about the call. Personally, I devised what I call my "points list," a scoring system to evaluate and compare each agent's services and attitude. It helped me gauge my reaction and keep my initial impressions straight. It also helped me realize if everything had been discussed—or if certain issues had been skirted.

After talking with all the agents on your list, look over those score sheets and decide which one impressed you the most. Send that person any material they asked to see. But don't ignore or forget the others you talked with.

As soon as you have reached an agreement with an agent, write the others friendly, business-like letters, explaining how nice it was to talk to them, but that you've engaged other representation and won't be sending them anything after all. Never leave anyone hanging. It's unprofessional.

If you cannot decide between two particular agents, and they haven't made an issue of "single submissions only," (i.e., an exclusive chance to review your work and to accept or reject it before you send it anywhere else), then yes, send your work to both. But in your cover letter, be clear that you are sending a simultaneous submission. That's all you need to say; you don't need to name the other agency. But always play fair.

Having had the presence of mind to ask each agent how long it will take to review your submission, wait several days *past* that time before making a follow-up call. Give the agent some leeway. If she says she'll have read your work by Friday, give her at least until the middle of the following week before calling her about it.

If, when she reads your submission, she decides on her end that maybe you weren't meant for each other after all, be gracious. Thank her for her time.

Then go back to your points list and see who scored second highest. Suddenly, that person looks even better! Send this next agent your work and continue from there.

Agent Comparison Checklist

This points list is a starting point to help you gauge which agent is best for you. Your priorities may differ from mine. But be consistent and clear in your own mind what you value most.

1. FEES & MONEY

_____ 10% *(5 points)*

_____ 15% until total fees reach a pre-agreed low breakpoint, then 10% thereafter *(3 points)*

_____ 15% with high breakpoint, then 10% *(2 points)*

_____ Flat 15% *(1 point)*

_____ Over 15% *(deduct 4 points)*

_____ Charges office costs *(deduct 2 points)*

2. PERSONALITY

_____ Interested to talk to me *(2 points)*

_____ Sounded friendly *(1-4 points)*

_____ Sounded enthusiastic *(1-6 points)*

_____ Asked *me* lots of questions *(2 points)*

_____ Laughed at least once *(1 point)*

_____ Sounded depressing *(deduct 2 points)*

3. PAYOUT

_____ Same-day turnaround *(6 points)*

_____ Next-day turnaround *(4 points)*

_____ 5-day turnaround *(2 points)*

_____ 10-day turnaround *(1 point)*

_____ Won't be specific *(deduct 5 points)*

4. BONUS POINTS

_____ Talked about career growth immediately *(1 point)*

_____ Works well with publishing houses I already like *(1 point)*

_____ Offered references without asking *(1 point)*

_____ Forwards copies of correspondence if asked *(2 points)*

_____ Informs about all telephone calls *(2 points)*

_____ Prefers a verbal agreement over contract *(2 points)*

_____ Glowing reports from those references checked *(2 points)*

_____ Attends conferences *(2 points)*

_____ Refused to give references *(deduct 1 point)*

5. SPECIAL CONSIDERATIONS

These are matters most important to me, in my experience. You may come up with other items and points.

_____ Has personal contacts for foreign rights *(10 points)*

_____ Has separate escrow account for royalties *(20 points)*

_____ Has a will that provides for keeping my earned royalties and works-under-consideration from being tied up in her estate in the unfortunate event of the agent's demise *(20 points)*

6. GRAND TOTAL (Total Score for this agent): _____

CHAPTER 33

An Conversation with an Agent

Interview with Natasha Kern
Natasha Kern Literary Agency

Rebecca Vinyard: What do you feel is the most common misconception authors have about agents?

Natasha Kern: The most common misconception is about what our job actually is in that we take these things and send them off, then wait for our chance to close the deal. They don't take into consideration not just the negotiation piece of it, but having to figure out if there are things to be done about publicity, or if the editor leaves, cover problems, title wars, distribution issues, royalty statements and legal problems.

There's a thousand other things that we also do as well—foreign rights, book-club rights, that kind of stuff.

Vinyard: Do you really think it matters if an agent has a prestigious New York address?

Kern: I used to live in New York and I have a lot of clients who live in New York, maybe almost a dozen now. Right now I have an African American client who lives in New York and is very well-connected to publishing there. He actually plays tennis with an agent there. I asked him—why did you pick an agent who lives in Oregon when you know several New York agents personally? Why not pick an African American agent, since there are several in New York? Without missing a beat, he said, "Gee, Natasha, you've always looked black to me!"

His point was he wouldn't pick an agent based on superficial criteria such as race or location. He wants someone who's gonna work for him, who is a champion for his work, who understands what he is doing, and who is going to get the job done. The fact that he knew other agents obviously gave him a choice.

What you are looking for is not an address. What you are looking for is someone who will be a champion for your work. Someone who is passionate about what *you're* doing.

Being on the West Coast has some huge advantages. Everything happens first here, so we tend to be very much on the cutting edge of things and know way before New York agents what things are actually sellable.

I think that people who live and work in New York also get caught up in the ethnocentrism of New York. They get a little bit out of touch with what the rest of the country is actually thinking about and reading.

Vinyard: That's a good point. I like that. Kind of along those same lines, what area or subgenre of the romance market do you think has the most potential right now?

Kern: Historicals are really coming back. Contemporaries have been all the rage for years. Chick lit isn't romance per se, but chick lit is still pretty strong, although some people are feeling like 'well, this is getting a little tiresome because there aren't any real characters arcs or any real plots and they're kinda like sitcom episodes.' So I guess there are some people who have issues about how long that will be a strong contender.

But I see that not only are historicals coming back, but with a broader venue rather than just English settings. And of course, the steamier books are being very much promoted by everybody. Everybody seems to be moving to steamier books.

Vinyard: Well, women usually say they like steamy over sweet. Although sometimes it's a little too steamy . . .

Kern: And it's way more so today. Maybe in an era of AIDS people have more of a vicarious sense of sexuality.

Vinyard: What do you look for in a prospective client's work? What sort of thing catches your eye?

Kern: The writing. The minute I read that first paragraph or two, I want to say, "Wow, this person can write." Usually my assistants will spot it when they first open that envelope and say, 'Hey, here's somebody that can really write.'

And they [the writer] may not know how to plot that well or they may not know character development, but they can learn those things if they actually have a writing gift or ability. The other things often take time to learn, sometimes years, but at least they have something to offer.

Vinyard: How should a new author approach your office? Should they send a query letter?

Kern: Yes, they should just send a query letter.

Vinyard: Does it matter if they are published or unpublished?

Kern: No, we look at everyone's work.

Section 5

Inspiration, Commiseration, and Information

CHAPTER 34

Coping With Rejection

YESTERDAY, I CALLED MY AGENT to check on the status of my latest submission. He said those words every writer dreads hearing, "It's on its way back to you, along with the rejection letters. Most of them said you're a good writer, but there isn't enough 'romance' in the story."

Did I cry? Wouldn't be professional. But as soon as I hung up, I called my best friend to tell her my tale of woe. She said, "Oh Becky, this is probably the best thing that's ever happened to you. We should go out and celebrate."

Celebrate?

No, my friend is *not* a sadistic, insensitive creep. She loves my work. But she (along with the rest of my critique group) considers what I write to be more mainstream than romance, and feels I should market it that way. So, in her opinion, this rejection is a good thing, because now I'll forget about submitting as a romance writer and present my work the way it should be presented.

Sigh. I listened . . . and agreed. But told her I was going to wallow around in self-pity for a day anyway.

That's my rule. I allow one day to wallow around in my hurt, to feel the pain of rejection at it's fullest, to be as self-indulgently sad as I want to be.

In the last four years (one year of submitting by myself, three via an agent), I've collected 53 rejection letters for five different novels. Sheer volume alone makes me something of an expert on coping with rejection. In the beginning, I was absolutely crushed. I did cry . . . a lot. Then I went through a period where instead of crying, I got angry. Either way, the emotions would throw me into a tailspin. I'd sit down to write, and the words wouldn't come. Why bother? I was a failure, right?

Wrong! Let me share a quote from science-fiction author, Ray Bradbury:

> If you write a hundred short stories, and they're all bad, it doesn't mean you're a failure. You only fail when you stop writing.

You only fail when you stop writing!

These are the most important words you'll ever read. Memorize them. Chant them silently to yourself every time you feel even the slightest doubt. No matter what anyone says, you only fail if you cease to try.

You might wonder what I did after I got off the phone with my best friend. Well . . . I switched on the computer . . . sat down . . . and I wrote.

I only wrote a page. But being able to do that, when the pain of rejection was like a bleeding wound in my heart, proved to myself, I am *not* a failure.

Then, I curled up with a good book and a box of chocolates. (I ate half the box!), After that, I took a long, hot bubble bath by candlelight with a glass of wine close by. In short, I pampered myself. I gave in to my every whim, because doggone it, I *deserve* it!

Let me tell you, it sure beats curling up in a ball on the bed, crying my eyes out. Today, I woke refreshed and ready to write. See? I'm writing right now!

That's what rejection is all about, learning from your mistakes, then starting over. My dear friend is right. Rejection *is* a good thing, because now I have a fresh start. It's the beginning of a new dream, not the end of an old one.

There are, of course, some practical considerations. Everyone will tell you if you want to be in this business, you need thick skin. I'd say mine is like alligator hide by now. But it is by no means easy; not everyone can stand the hurt rejection brings.

I've known authors who gave up after getting one rejection on a single submission. Don't sell yourself short like that, please. You deserve better than that.

So here are a few of my coping tips. I hope these will help when you need to take a painful experience and turn it into a learning opportunity.

- Only read your rejection letter *once*, then set it aside for a few days.

- After a couple of days, go back and read the letter. Try to see the editor's opinions with an objective eye. Sit down and make a list of how you can improve your writing next time.

- Set a new goal. Do you want to rewrite this book? Do you want to submit it somewhere else? Or is it time to move on to another story? Only you can decide this one for yourself.

- Do something nice for yourself.

- Save your rejections.

I'll bet the last one has you thinking, *what?* Save my rejections? You gotta be kidding!

No, I'm serious. How do I know I have 53 letters on file? Because I started saving them when I was submitting on my own, without an agent. I wanted to keep track of which editors liked my work more than others, so I could target them when I got around to submitting the next book.

For there *is* such a thing as a positive rejection letter. Keep them all. They are valuable not only as learning tools, but also as marketing tools.

Rejections also make great motivators. When I made my first sale, what do you think I did? I spread all my rejections out on the floor, popped open a bottle of champagne, and I *danced* on them!

You might have a more creative fantasy; one author told me she was hoping to find a way to use her letters to make voodoo dolls of certain editors. . . .

The point is, you should use your rejections as a means to continue on toward your publication goals. You *can* gain from the pain.

You only fail if you stop writing.

CHAPTER 35

Writing the Inspirational Novel

by Ruth Scofield Schmidt

I'VE WRITTEN FIVE contemporary romance novels for Steeple Hill, the inspirational imprint of Harlequin-Silhouette, and have a contract for a sixth. And I've discovered that there are still many writers who don't quite understand what an "inspirational" is.

At a recent conference in Chicago, I sat at lunch with a beginning writer who, out of the blue, asked me, "Do you have to believe all that stuff to sell it?"

I chewed my mouthful of food for about five seconds and studied the woman's expression. Her "all that stuff" had held a tiny sliver of contempt.

But I sensed she wanted an honest answer, so I swallowed quickly so I could speak without garbling my answer.

"It sure helps," I told her. "If you don't believe in what you're writing, that will come through. Readers will know it."

And they will.

What exactly is an inspirational? How does it differ from other romances?

An inspirational romance novel will contain three threads:

1. The heroine's life and what she wants out of it

2. The hero's life and what he wants out of it

3. Spiritual growth. Showing the faith that is either already there, or is born, that becomes an integral part of these lives.

All three threads are woven together as two people fall in love while they work out their personal conflicts in life. The one key difference between an inspirational and any other romance novel: Even though the story will show sexual tension between hero and heroine, the consummation of their love stays behind closed doors and after marriage.

All other elements of a good romance remain in inspirationals.

1. First and last, the story must entertain the reader.

2. Characters have to have full, sympathetic development. The reader should empathize with the heroine and fall in love with the hero.

3. Plot has to move the story along, carrying the reader to "The End" without pause.

4. The sexual tension must be strong throughout, leading to emotional satisfaction for the heroine and hero in their union at the end.

5. The happy ending is a must, leaving the reader with a sigh of contentment and eager to read your next book.

6. Finally, a romance novel is first and foremost a personal relationship story between a man and woman. In inspirations, so too must it be for the protagonists and God. Relationships are, after all, what life is all about.

Who is the audience for this kind of a read? Yes, our readers are mostly Christian. Church-goers. Old, young, and in-between. Believers from all denominations and life experiences. Yet, we often find readers outside this experience who enjoy the inspirational novel as well—readers who are seeking a gentle read. And yes, these readers like having the thrill of a romance and a good tale without going past the bedroom door.

Writing about relationships is my primary business. Creating a story with a relationship between my heroine and hero and God is, in my opinion, to share life's finest riches. Showing the spiritual growth in them enriches who they are. I like showing them in full living color with all three dimensions: mind, body, and spirit. My audience likes seeing them that way too.

Does an author have to believe in God to write a successful inspirational novel? I say yes. Knowing God, not just about Him, is what gives this type of work its authenticity. This above all other story elements has to ring true in an inspirational novel. Without a doubt, I am sure that other Christian authors will agree with me on that.

CHAPTER 36

Writing the Paranormal Romance

by Connie Flynn

S O YOU WANT TO WRITE a paranormal romance? It would seem easy enough. Just write a regular romance and throw in a supernatural character or element and there you go.

If only this were true.

Pitfalls abound when you write about the supernatural, and if you don't understand what they are, your novel will fall flat. I make no claims that this brief article is a complete primer, but I will attempt to pass on some major "do's" for writing the successful paranormal romance.

1. Create a supernatural world.

Supernatural worlds have freedoms and limitations, both physical and cultural, just like the ordinary world. These freedoms and limitations must find their basis in a believable system of logic that relates to the world of the reader. So, just as our culture evolved from believing airplane flight was impossible to anticipating eventual flight to nearby planets, you build your story and its world by revealing one "known fact" after the other until it all seems possible.

2. Once you've built your story world's rules of logic, follow them without fail.

Your ghost walks through walls with ease and also picks up objects with equal ease. How? A being insubstantial enough to pass through solid matter should have a hard time wrapping its ephemeral hand around a lamp. Such leaps in logic must be powerfully justified.

Likewise, watch out for unexplained fairy dust that just happens to let your flightless dragon spout wings. Instead, better that the creature has to practice, take magic potions, go to a magician, pray . . . whatever it takes. Then and only then can it soar in the mountaintops.

When you build and follow your story logic faithfully, you create suspension of disbelief and as long as you adhere to the logic, the reader will follow you anywhere.

3. Build vulnerability into the supernatural characters.

Without it, the story has no balance of power and, therefore, no conflict. The vulnerability can be physical or come from an ethical viewpoint. If Superman were invincible, his writers would be hard put to find worthy opponents. So they invented Kryptonite. They then took it even further by giving him a strong sense of justice and a desire to get close to people he loves, making him additionally vulnerable to those without his scruples or loyalty. Thus we have a powerful hero who can still be brought down.

Do the same with your supernatural villains. Vampires sleep by day, making them vulnerable in their coffins. Demons, werewolves, and devils must also have these soft underbellies. Invent vulnerabilities, stay true to them, then let your less powerful characters struggle to discover what they are and, in that discovery, find the means to prevail.

4. Put your protagonist through a period of disorientation before he or she accepts the supernatural occurrence.

Too often, a character thrust into a supernatural situation just appears to say, "Oh, yeah . . . okay," and immediately adjusts to the new reality. The reader is left feeling uneasy, and often doesn't know why.

What's wrong is the lack of character re-orientation. When a person's accepted reality (and self-image) is threatened, they go through the five stages of grief—denial, anger, bargaining, depression (or resentful resignation), then finally acceptance. This can happen rapidly or take place over time.

And it's a very tricky area of writing paranormal. Take too long and readers might think the character is slow on the uptake. Be too quick and you will get accused of resorting to author convenience. Achieving the right balance depends in part on perceiving the relative presence of the supernatural aspects of the novel. When the supernatural element is in-your-face, the transition must be fast. If the element is more subtle or more removed from the character, acceptance must come slower.

5. Decide how you'll get the hero and heroine together before you begin.

Romance readers expect you to bring the hero and heroine together in the end—permanently. This isn't unduly challenging when the protagonists come from the same world and are facing the supernatural together. But when one of them comes from the supernatural world, you've got your hands full. How do you pair up a ghost, angel, werewolf, or time- or space-traveler with a person outside that world?

Obviously, one character must give up his or her former world. In the ghost story, your ghost must become alive again . . . or the human character must die. The angel must become mortal . . . or, again, the human character must die. The werewolf or vampire must be redeemed . . . or the other character must become one.

Only time- or space-travel offer any flexibility in solving this dilemma; the other realities are problematic at best and a set-up for a disappointing ending at worst. Turning your mortal character into a werewolf or vampire will work only if you make that world appealing enough for readers to believe the character (and, indeed, even themselves) would make such a choice.

The prospect of an angel giving up heaven isn't much more appealing than having the mortal character die. And while you can bring a ghost alive, or substitute a look-alike living person, readers often feel cheated by such endings. The same is true if you have a higher power intervene; it robs the characters of the opportunity to solve their own problems.

There are no pat solutions to this inherent problem, only the warning: You must set the stage for the resolution long before you write the book. Foreshadow it. Give clues. Make one character so profoundly dissatisfied with his or her former life that leaving it behind seems the better choice. Or give the supernatural character some sort of significant unfinished business in the ordinary world.

If you don't plan ahead, you'll be tempted to take the easy way, such as making a character go against type or bringing in the powerful wizard. And this really makes readers mad.

6. Remember, you're writing a romance.

It's easy to become so fascinated with your story world and its supernatural characters that you forget the romance. So while you're having all this imaginative and supernatural fun, remember to make your new world enhance the romance plot. Let the uncertainty of the supernatural events force the characters together—even as it creates friction and mistrust between them.

Otherwise, you may be writing a damn fine paranormal novel with a romantic sub-plot, but you aren't writing a romance.

What I find most exciting about writing paranormal romances is the chance to create my own world. You probably do, too, which is what drew you to the sub-genre in the first place. Just remember to keep these principles in mind, invent some of your own, and, most of all, have fun creating a world that never was.

CHAPTER 37

10 Ways To Survive Between Sales

by Rachelle Nelson Morgan

AFTER FINISHING MY THIRD historical for Jove, sold in January 1996 and completed that May, I began counting the months. A total of seventeen months passed before getting that next dizzying call from my agent, "They want to buy . . ."

At first, the extended time following that sale left me feeling isolated, insecure, and somehow a failure. I had many friends that did their best to encourage me. But there were times when it seemed that nothing that anyone could do or say could keep my spirits up. I tried not to burden my friends with my discouragement.

Instead, I came up with a list of ten things to make the most of my time and help me survive those tough, frustrating, clock-ticking months.

1. *Read*. Make a dent in Mount To-Be-Read. Not only does this help revitalize those creative juices, but it helps you become more familiar with what is being released currently by romance publishers. It also helps to reduce the guilt you might feel for not reading that book or books you've been planning to read for ages.

2. *Research.* Read broadly—read books of fiction and nonfiction, magazines, old newspapers, novellas, mini-mags. Make notes of each little tidbit that strikes your fancy. Watch television shows, movies, and documentaries. (The show I watched about tigers helped to inspire *Wild Cat Cait*—I also discovered later it had inspired other authors who had watched the same show!)

   Take trips (even short ones). Attend chapter meetings and conferences. Go people-watching, visit friends, cruise the Internet. Being under contract for a novel leaves little time to do more than sit at the work-desk and create. You've got a break; put it to good use.

3. *Family time.* Your family misses you when you're working, especially when a deadline keeps you chained to the computer. Spend time with your husband, your children, your parents, grandparents. This can range from doing yard work together to taking longer vacations.

4. *Rest, relax.* Do something you've always wanted to do, but haven't had time to tackle. Make that rabbit cage. Redecorate a room. Put in a garden. Look for things that give your mind a rest from writing and creating. This is a great time to let your batteries recharge.

5. *Proposals.* When relaxing drives you crazy, write. Churn out those proposals, one after the other. Any given one might not fit a house's current needs, but a second or third might. I managed to put together seven solid proposals in my "off-time."

6. *Chapter Involvement.* This activity keeps you busy and close to the business. Volunteer for anything from being a hostess to coordinating a contest to serving on the board. As a published author, you can help mentor others. At the same time, it puts you into contact with people from other chapters, the media, and publishing houses.

   These networks of relationships, focused now on chapter work, may stand you in good stead later. All of this community involvement also helps you hone your public-relation skills.

7. *Get Organized.* Clean out your computer files, cabinets or paper files, research articles, and magazine stacks. Make or update your databases of readers and booksellers. Put together a scrapbook—this is a

great way to indulge in rereading good reviews and fan mail. Get prepared for that next bout of deadline dementia, when the piles start forming again and the shelves once more collect dust.

8. *Revise.* Bring out old manuscripts or work that has been rejected. Given what you know now, is the work salvageable? If so, put your knowledge and experience to good use. If not, revert to Tip #5 above.

9. *Attend conferences.* Choose carefully from those that can help your current situation. Meet influential people in the business. Refresh your mind with techniques you may have forgotten; any workshop has the potential to spark your creativity or teach you something new!

10. *Write articles.* Take what you've learned and put it to paper. Turn something negative into something positive.

If can't think of enough information to fill a full article, try posing a question to other authors. By compiling their responses into an article, you not only share their knowledge but also give them a bit of publicity. Maybe they'll find a way to reciprocate.

Articles are a great way to keep your name out there between sales. They don't have to be ten pages long—sometimes, the shorter the better. Start by looking to your chapter, other chapters, writing magazines, or on the Internet for newsletters and websites that need articles. Believe me, as a former newsletter editor, original articles are always welcome.

Being a writer means becoming familiar with the natural flexibility of workloads, the cycles of markets, and variety of intense periods of writing under deadline interspersed with more open, relaxed times.

In the more open-ended periods, enjoy the variety of these optional pursuits. They will refresh and recharge your creative powers. Keep a positive attitude, and work on your skills, networks, market knowledge, and general state of readiness.

Before you know it, that next major project will appear. And you'll be happy you spent this time getting ready to write that next great novel in your career.

CHAPTER 38

Author Websites & Online Promotion

Today, just about everybody and their cat has a website. For authors, websites and mailing lists have become a very essential part of book promotion.

How popular are these author websites? A couple years ago, the *Romance Writers Report* stated that the average author website receives about a hundred hits per month. That seems low to me. Trust me, you can do better than that. You don't have to be a bestselling author to have a successful website. All you need is to put a little thought and planning into content, design, and promotion.

Hosting options and Web addresses

Let's start with where your site will exist and what "address" it will have, because that's half the battle. You need to think about website promotion at all times. How will people learn about your site and find their way to it? The first thing to consider is your site's URL (Universal Resource Locator). Here are three options:

1. Your best bet, if you can afford it, is to register your own "domain name"— for example, http://rebeccavinyard.com. Domain names in-

volve some costs; you have to pay domain registration fees every year, for the rights to that name.

You'll also need a web "host" that runs that website—i.e., provides space and maintains the underlying technological workings for that unique site.

Prices can range upwards from $10/month for the host services, and $35/year for registering your domain name. My feeling is that it's worth it to plunk down the money so that you can get name recognition and so that readers can find your site easily.

2. If these fees aren't in your budget, then consider web space with an established author hosting site. These are places that specialize in author websites, and keep them all routed to their domain name, with a suffix (usually your name) to locate your batch of pages on their group site.

    For some hosts, the drawback is that they don't allow you to access your files directly to update them. Instead, you pay the house designers to update your site for you. If you go this route, don't be shy about contacting the company's other clients first, to ask if they are satisfied with their web host.

    On the plus side, a group site can often get more hits because it offers a wider range of authors and content to attract visitors, who then may browse around a little. Also, these sites can have mailing lists and/or might organize special events (such as chats or contests) to promote your work.

    URLs for hosted websites will usually look something like this: http://rebeccavinyard.romance-central.com. Or it may look like: http://romance-central.com/rebeccavinyard with your name at the end. In either case, your name is still part of the URL.

3. The most economical (cheapest!) option is to go with an ISP (Internet Service Provider) web space or free web-space servers. Most ISPs include web space as part of their service. These are the folks that provide your home Internet connection, allowing you to have e-mail and browse the web. With your e-mail account, you may get the ability to create a website, which is maintained on their server.

One drawback is that some are sticky about content, so you might not be able to post that extra-hot love scene. Or they might view your page as a business site—and want to charge you extra for your account. It depends on the company.

Free web space is out there, but I don't recommend it. You'll have to put up with banner ads, pop-up ads, embedded icons—things the free-space host sells to increase their ad revenue. Also, the free-space servers tend to get overloaded a *lot*. An overloaded server means your pages might take forever to load, if they load at all.

With either an ISP or free space URL, chances are your name won't be anywhere in the address. Most ISPs assign a URL based on your user or login name or something entirely different.

For instance, my old Geocities (now owned by Yahoo) URL was: http://www.geocities.com/ Athens/Acropolis/2801/. Takes a lot of concentration to type that, doesn't it? This is not what you want for your promotional web address.

Ideally, the URL should include your name. Some authors have chosen to use the title of one of their book as their URL. Another option is to pay a little extra and register both—using the best of both worlds—and have your book-title URL redirect visitors to your name URL.

A similar approach is to use a service that redirects visitors to your free-space or ISP-hosted site using a unique domain-name URL.

Study your options. There are a few good books and resources on the web that offer advice for authors on creating websites. Ask others how they did it. Visit author websites you like, and note how they are set-up.

The goal is to figure out how you can get the most bang for your promotional buck.

Keywords and meta tags

After finding your home on the web, the next thing to think about in designing your site is "meta tags." What are these?

Meta tags are invisible bits of information embedded into your web page's code. They are important, because they contain keywords and site descriptions. These are things your visitors can't see, but search engine "spiders" can. Spiders are programs that search websites for keywords and site descriptions. For instance, if a user types "romance novel" in a search engine box and your site uses this as a keyword, then your site will be listed in the search results, provided you've registered with the search engine.

If you have meta tags embedded into your web page, the odds of people finding your site increase dramatically. Keep in mind not all spiders collect information the same way. Some collect only keywords. Some collect keywords and site descriptions. And some do all that *and* collect the first few lines of visible text on the page. That being the case, it behooves you to put some thought into the opening words that greet your visitors. (We'll look more at content questions below.)

Some designers think that repeating the same keywords over and over will raise the site's ranking with the search engines. The opposite is true. Some engines interpret oft-repeated keywords as "spamming the index" and may actually drop your site completely from their listings. Another tactic that doesn't work is using dozens of different keywords. Most spiders only collect the first twenty-five keywords. The same goes for site descriptions.

So put some thought into your meta tags. What words might the average person type into a search engine to find you and your writing?

Of course, you want to increase those hits that search engines provide, right? To do that, submit your site directly to the search engines. While there are software programs that claim they submit to hundreds of search engines all at once, my feeling is they are over-hyped and over-priced. Think about your own Internet usage. How many search engines do *you* use?

I think your best bet is to submit your site to the most popular search engines directly, and do it yourself. It's not hard. Go to their main pages and look for a "submit a URL" or "add URL" link. Then just follow their instructions. Some engines will add your site within 24 hours. Some will take weeks or months. Some might not ever add your site at all! Such are the mysterious ways of search engines.

Yes, most search engines will improve your site's placement if you buy ad space. But beware, this ad space doesn't come cheap.

Visual design

Next, let's talk about your site's appearance. If you are creating the site yourself, you have three options for graphics:

1. Buy them from a graphic designer or a web art program.

2. Use free graphics (there are countless free graphics sites out there).

3. Make them yourself, using a graphics program.

Whatever option you choose, use graphics and colors that either reflect your personality or compliment your book covers. The background and pictures should be pleasing to the eye and the text easy to read.

Here are some things to keep in mind:

1. Design. Keep it simple. A simple, well-organized design is generally more attractive and effective than a jumbled, busy one.

2. Computer speed. Complicated designs and lots of web-gizmos mean each page will take longer to load on the viewer's computer. Remember, many users still have older computers. The worst websites are sometimes done by those with the fanciest, newest computers. They forget how long an over-designed page can take to load on an less up-to-date (but still perfectly functional!) unit.

3. Viewer impatience. Viewers don't want to wait long for pages full of graphics to load. Some studies have shown that people only tend to spend a certain amount of time viewing any website. Do you want them to spend that time reading about you and you work, and maybe looking at a few selected photos? Or waiting and drumming their fingers in annoyance as those 40 photos from your summer trip, slowly load, one . . . by one . . . by one?

Keep it clean, fast, and let your visitors focus on what's important: getting to know you, your work, and your life. Don't try to overwhelm them with your designer skills. It's not what you're selling!

Content

Okay, you're a writer, so here's the question you should feel the most comfortable with. What kind of content is your site going to have? You'll want to list your book information and a bio—but what else? Sure, you want to sell your books. But to do that, you also have to sell yourself.

The *best* author sites are interactive. Readers love to interact with their favorite authors via scheduled chats, message boards, contests, and mailing lists. Offer these features and your visitors will be more likely to visit your site again and again.

Readers also love to find out what their favorite authors do when they *aren't* writing! They want to get to know you as a person. So if you have a hobby or want to show off those pictures of your cat, don't be afraid to do that. Just make sure this isn't the first thing readers see.

The first page is very important. What will the visitor see first? Some authors feel it's best to put the book information right up front, and then follow with subsequent sections with their bio, favorite links, and so on. Others put themselves first, usually with a small picture and a friendly greeting, followed by the book information. I prefer the latter, to help establish a relationship between the author and readers. In any event, make your first page friendly, but also full of real information.

It's always a good idea to include a link to an excerpt from your book on the front page, as well.

One simple concept: your first page should deliver a good idea of the kind of things to be found on the site. Think of visual orderliness; try to provide clear words and phrases. The general categories that navigate people to the other areas of the site are valuable to new visitors. It's like going shopping and entering a store. You want a simple directory that lets you know what aisle to check for something you might be interested in.

Think of the first page as a kind of visual map or directory, as well as a welcome page. One tip: don't get too cute. If you want people to find your bio, call it "Bio" or "About the Author." Calling it "Once Upon a Time" or something vague like that will just confuse. And confusion means people will leave your site and go elsewhere, quickly.

You would like a visitor to be able to find and get to where they wish to go in just a few clicks—three or four at most. Write out your plan on paper first, and show it to a few friends. Or better, corral a few near-strangers who don't yet know all about you and your writing—and ask them for feedback. Especially about your first page.

Your site should be easy to navigate—there should be links or buttons that guide your visitors easily throughout. Don't make them have to hit that back button—please. If you offer a mailing list or message board or chat room on your site, make sure it easily accessible from the front page.

Out of the three features listed above, a mailing list is probably the most productive in terms of promotion (and the least time-consuming). The easiest way to set one up is to use a mailing list service, like Yahoo Egroups.

Most authors only use their mailing lists to announce book signings and new releases. Others prefer a monthly newsletter format, to keep readers posted on what their favorite author is doing. Whether you're sweating out a deadline or taking a trip to Nepal, don't overlook the newsletter format to keep your name and your books in your readers' minds.

How about contests? Or giveaways? As a webmaster, I've monitored many contests for my clients. The ones that get the best response usually offer more than an autographed book. People love to get free stuff. So consider adding a gift basket or bookstore gift certificate—or maybe an item that relates to your book—to your prize list. You'll get more interested parties that way.

Promotion

Let's say you have your site built. Other than submitting it regularly to the search engines, what can you do to attract visitors? Below is a list of sure-fire ways to promote your books online.

1. Visit other sites related to your genre and ask for a link exchange.

2. Submit your book to online book review sites.

3. Write articles for sites on writing (trust me, webmasters are *always*

desperate for content!) in exchange for a promotional link.

4. Do online interviews and offer yourself up as a guest star for chats.

5. Buy ad space with e-zines and online newsletters. (These can be relatively inexpensive for text-only ads.)

6. The easiest and most overlooked form of online promotion is e-mail. Set up a signature file for your e-mails that includes your URL, book title, and release date information. This way every time you send an e-mail, you promote your book, too.

7 Add your URL to your business cards and promotional bookmarks.

8. Ask your publisher to include your URL with your bio in the book.

9. If you do speaking engagements or book signings, include your URL in your handouts.

Remember, there's a real world out there. Online promotion is an effective tool, but there's no substitute for a handshake and a smile. Still, a good website is an important component of marketing your work. It will give your name stronger recognition, deepen your relationships with fans, and introduce new readers to your work.

CHAPTER 39

Alternative Publishing

I F YOU'VE WRITTEN A BOOK that gets positive rejections (nice comments but rejected nonetheless), and can't find a niche with traditional print publishers, you might consider alternative publishing. There are several options available these days—electronic publishing, print-on-demand publishing, web publishing, and subsidy and self-publishing.

For new authors trying to crack into the traditional market in a roundabout way, or established authors that want to sell their out-of-print backlist or new books in a genre that doesn't interest their current publishers, non-traditional publishing might be an option.

Let's take a brief look at these alternatives.

Electronic publishing or E-books

The market for e-books has huge potential, but has yet to reach the masses. E-books are available via electronic downloads (delivered over the Internet to your computer), or on discs and CDs. They can be read via specialized e-book readers, on computers, or printed out.

Some traditional publishers have recognized the potential benefits in lower production costs and no warehousing, and have made tentative forays into the e-book market. But problems persist. One is finding a standard electronic format; most e-publishers have adopted the OEB standard (open e-book standard), but some still rely on Adobe's PDF.

Another is the high cost of e-book readers, the handheld devices that display and store electronic text. Until these issues are sorted out, this market can't reach its full potential.

Print-on-Demand Publishing

This is a method of printing books one at a time. As the name indicates, this allows publishers to print literally "on demand" as they print only a small number at a time, then reprint as needed in small quantities. POD is done via digitally formatted text on laser printing systems. It allows publishers to forgo the traditional print runs of several thousand books, thus eliminating problems of warehousing and returns from bookstores.

The problem is the expense involved, due to the technology and the extra costs to print smaller numbers of books a time. A print-on-demand book costs more per unit than a book using a standard print run. Still, this is an interesting approach, and in theory allows publishers to test titles before committing to large print runs.

Most sources agree the costs will go down over time, as more publishers and retailers invest in their own machines and learn how to calculate the best ways to use these opportunities.

One interesting approach being tested is installing book-at-a-time machines in bookstores, or in places like airports or warehouse mega-stores. Customers can search the database for the title they want, and print it out "on demand"—with a softcover binding and full-color cover—in just a few minutes.

Web Publishing

Putting it up on the web? Well, this is hardly a new idea, but it is good to remember this is a form of "publishing," which really means to make available to the public. There is still a strong demand for web content.

Formats change and develop over time. HTML format is still the standard, but XML has been gaining popularity, as it allows users to download content onto portable devices.

Subsidy and Self-Publishing

Subsidy publishing is not my favorite choice, since it means you, the author, pay for part of or all of the publishing costs. This lowers the risk factor for the publisher to just about nil, and allows them to accept manuscripts that other publishers consider bad investments.

And you are likely to get precious little editorial help, which is one of the most valuable services a new author gets from working with a traditional publisher. Furthermore, the amount of promotion that subsidy-published books receive varies widely. While some companies do support their authors, others come very close to being scam artists.

If you choose to go the self-publishing route, on the other hand, be prepared to do a lot of learning. There are good published resources on self-publishing as a business endeavor. It can be done—and done successfully.

But it requires a lot of work, plus careful preparation of a well-planned budget that doesn't overlook all the hidden costs involved.

Pros and cons

As you can see, there are some risks involved in taking the alternative publishing route. Let's examine the pros and cons.

PRO: Royalties are generally higher. Electronic publishers usually offer 25-50% as opposed to the traditional print publishers' 10-15%.

CON: Very few alternative publishers pay advances. The higher royalty rate is designed to reflect that. But if your sales are low, you're not going to make much on royalties. Let's face it, 10% royalty on thousands of copies sold is better than 50% on a few dozen sold.

PRO: Authors have more input into the marketing and packaging of their work, compared to traditional publishers.

CON: Most of these alternative companies have small publicity budgets. The more entrepreneurial ones will often place a few ads in trade magazines and send out copies for review. But too often, authors must manage and cover much of the promotion and promotional expenses.

PRO: Romance is the number one genre for alternative publishing, with science fiction and horror right behind it. And most of these publishers are set up to sell direct via websites and 800-numbers.

CON: Bookstore distribution channels are still limited for these alternative publishers. A few independents have contracts with major distributors, but this is usually limited to making their titles available through direct orders (often requiring a customer to first go into a store, request the book, place an order, and wait for delivery before they can pick it up), rather than broader placement on store shelves for browsing customers.

PRO: Alternative publishers are open to a wide variety of stories. Subjects that are taboo with traditional publishers are welcomed and, in some cases, encouraged.

CON: You're looking at reaching a smaller reading audience.

PRO: Most electronic publishers allow the author to retain the rights to hard-copy printed editions. This means a writer can still continue to submit the story to traditional outlets.

CON: Many traditional publishers now include electronic rights in their standard contracts, which makes a previously e-published book harder to sell in the print market.

PRO: Many e-published and POD authors have already established their own loyal fan bases. And the number of readers of electronic and POD books has been steadily growing.

CON: *R-E-S-P-E-C-T!* Don't be surprised if some people dismiss an e-book as being "not a real book." The perception is that alternative publishers are not as selective as their traditional print cousins. However, as readerships continue to grow and as the quality of e-books and POD books continues to prove itself—some have won major awards or have gone on to be picked up by the same traditional publishers that initially rejected them—this perception will hopefully change.

You may think I'm little biased on this subject, since I've had two books electronically published, with three more under contract. But in some ways I feel I'm in a position to be objective because I've experienced (and witnessed) both the pros and cons of electronic publishing.

The bottom line: do your homework first. Before approaching an alternative publisher, be smart and research them thoroughly.

Some tips on what to look for:

1. How long has the company been in business? If it's an established company (I'd recommend at least three years in the business) with a long, solid backlist, they will be a better choice than a new, unproven company. Over the years, I've seen many electronic publishers come and go, sometimes tying up dozens of authors' works in contracts only to go out of business without warning. You don't want to find yourself a victim of that scenario. So look for an e-publisher with a proven track record and loyal customer base.

2. Does the company charge a fee? Most reputable e-publishers do *not* charge authors a fee for publication costs. Most will, of course, charge an author for books the author chooses to buy. But it should be optional to buy books, not required.

    In the case of POD, there are some publishers that require the author to pay a nominal set-up and/or maintenance fee to offset those costs. Nominal is the key word here. If your investment is going to put a big dent in your checkbook, think twice before signing on the dotted line. And shop around.

3. Do they have open contracts? Many electronic publishers have their contracts posted on their websites. Most ask only for the e-rights and keep them for a limited time, one to three years perhaps, after which time those rights should revert to you without action. The contracts should allow for cancellation of the contract by request. If an electronic publisher also does POD books, there is often a separate contract for each format.

4. Do they have in-house editing? A red flag should go up if the publisher relies only on the author for editing. Frankly, this means they care little about the quality of the books they sell. Publishers should have experience in editing and marketing, and be able to turn out a professional product. And if the covers of the other books in their program look shoddy, beware.

5. What formats do they use? Since there are a wide variety of formats available, it's good if the publisher uses as many as possible. If they limit themselves to one format, then they are limiting the number of potential readers.

6. What kind of promotion do they offer? The best companies promote their books in a variety of ways—via trade magazines, sending copies or files out for review, and direct marketing to mailing lists. The company's website should look professional and be easy to navigate and shop for the books online. If it doesn't, think twice about how well your books will sell.

7. What do their authors say about them? Don't be shy—ask! Usually, there are links back to the authors' websites or e-mail addresses. Drop the authors a line to ask how they feel about the company.

Ultimately, the choice of whether or not to go with alternative publishing is up to you. Just make sure your choice is an informed one.

CHAPTER 40

Conversation with an E-publisher

Interview with Dick Claassen
Awe-Struck E-Books

Rebecca Vinyard: Tell us a bit about yourself and Awe-Struck E-Books.

Dick Claassen: My partner Kathryn Struck and I are first cousins, so we've known each other and been good friends for many years. We're also both—sharing the same genes across the family line—driven to succeed. It's both a gift and a curse to be this way. It's a gift because of what I think we've accomplished in digital publishing; it's a curse on those days we're so tired we can hardly function.

Contrary to what most people think, you can't just put up a website and watch the money come rolling in. You have to work just as hard as if you were running a bricks-and-mortar store. In some ways, harder. The saying, "There ain't no such thing as a free lunch," never meant more than it does in this business.

Vinyard: What do you feel is the most common misconception about electronic publishing?

Claassen: There are several misconceptions, as I see it. The most irritating—to me, anyway—is that people think the caliber of digital content is lower than in-print content. Have you ever read a really *bad* book in print? I know I have. I've read lots of really terrible books in print.

In fact, the terrible books I've read encouraged me to write my own novels. I would sit there with a bad book and think, "I can do better than this. I can write better than this." Of course, a person doesn't just start writing and out pops a novel. I've been writing all my life. It takes practice to discover how to put words together.

But it was the bad in-print content that made me want to start writing my own stories in the first place. And now we (Awe-Struck) publish the stories of more than a hundred very fine authors.

The second misconception is that if you have your book published digitally, it forever ruins your chances to ever have a big "tree-publisher" snap up your book. Come on! As Dr. Phil would say, "Did you have dumb flakes for breakfast?"

Words are words, regardless of how they might be delivered to our brains. Digital books are as legitimate as any book in print. I suspect this particular "fact" of ruining your chances with a big tree-publisher was floated by those who want e-books to fail. But e-books won't. They're already here. And they're not going away.

Vinyard: Do you foresee a universal format for e-books?

Claassen: I *so* wish there was a universal format. Mary Taffs, our extremely hard-working production coordinator, puts each title we publish into 10 different formats.

That's a lot of work for one title. Before Mary makes those ten e-book incarnations, I have to make the graphic cover packages—each a different size, or on a different template, or both.

So Mary and I would like to see just one format. I'm surprised that Bill Gates didn't get his way with his .lit format. I still think it's a strong contender if the dust ever starts to settle. Another strong contender is Adobe's PDF. PDF has the most power in its presentation, being able to display graphics, tables, complex formatting, etc.

We'll see. There are so many devices now that display e-books, with each device demanding a different format, the jury is still out because no one wants to give up their own pet format.

Vinyard: How does Awe-Struck E-Books promote their books and their authors?

Claassen: Well, there are the search engines, of course. I register each new description page of a title with around 60 or 70 search engines. Kathryn runs online ads on a regular basis. Our distributors are valuable promoters just by their nature. Barnes and Noble, Fictionwise, Powell's, etc., post our books on their sites, and they also use keywords in their own site search engines to lead potential customers to our books.

Some of our authors do a fair amount of promoting. All of this works together, but I suspect that search-engine registration is still the most powerful promo tool we have. What do you do when you go online? You probably go to places like Google. So we'll continue to register our pages there.

Vinyard: What sort of stories are on your wish list?

Claassen: Anything that's interesting and well-written. We're after superior content. We have offerings in romance, sci fi, sci-fi romance, historical, mainstream, nonfiction, and New Age. My personal favorite is sci-fi romance, because I write my own novels in this genre and I appreciate a good love story with an interesting sci-fi plot.

I love books. I love good writing. And I love to read those good books on my Palm Pilot. How convenient can it get? You can have 20 books on just one small device you hold in your hand!

People don't understand the wonderful convenience of e-books. The PDAs (Palm, Sony Clie, Pocket PC, eBookman, Hiebook, Softbook, etc.) even have their own back lights so you can read in the dark! And prices are heading down.

E-books are here. Print is by no means the media of the past. But e-books are the media of the future. So if you have a PDA with an e-book on it, you're already holding the future in your hot little hand.

CHAPTER 41

Writing the Story of Your Heart

S O MANY WORKSHOPS AND ARTICLES focus on writing to sell. After all, that's what successful writers do: Sell their books. Right? So it stands to reason a person should write what sells. So you study the market. You listen to experts. You try to write the most marketable work you can. This, many people will tell you, is the key to success.

But is success the key to happiness?

I'm not too sure about that.

Every writer wants to be successful. They dream of people loving their words as much as they do. And they dream that their love of words will bring them financial freedom.

You can picture it, can't you? Waking in the morning in your dream house ... walking to your dream office ... and sitting down to work on your next bestseller. Your publisher promotes your book on national TV. People flock to your book signings. Readers send you bags of fan mail.

Well, I hate to burst your bubble, but only a rarefied collection of writers achieve this kind of success. Your average published author still has to worry about paying their mortgages and bills, about keeping their place on their publisher's book lists, about promoting their work. Their books aren't advertised on TV. They feel lucky if their publisher deigns to pony up for a lousy magazine ad. And if ten people show up at their book signings, they're thrilled.

Are these average published authors happy? Perhaps. But if you asked most of them if publishing a book was the key to happiness, I'm sure many would say, "No, you're wrong." Especially if you asked those who feel locked into a specific genre or storytelling style, you'd find too often the joy of writing has been replaced by the job of writing.

Joy equals job? A lopsided equation if I ever saw one. As someone who has tried to live by these numbers, I can definitely say the second one often cancels out the first.

Why am I telling you this, you ask? For years, I've been writing articles to encourage writers. Now, am I doing the opposite? Not really. In this current era of reality television shows, let's just call this a "reality" article.

Selling a book might be your dream. For me, it's still the best dream around. Keeping your head in the clouds might get you underway. But to survive the ride, you need your feet on the ground.

Publishing is a *tough* business. One year, you might be your editor's darling. The next … your editor is at a different publishing house, and your new one decides she wants to take the company in a different direction, a new strategy that doesn't include you.

Think I'm being too negative? Plenty of published authors will tell you I'm going easy on the whole matter. Publishing is at best a capricious business. So much depends on having the right book on the desk of the right person at the right time.

At worst, let's face it, it can be a demeaning business. You write what you are convinced you need to write to keep your job.

My favorite question to ask published authors is "Which book is the story of your heart"? It's an amazing question. Invariably, the author's face will light up, as she gladly tells you all about *that* book. She smiles and gets animated, as she tells you why the story meant so much to her. How easy it was to write because the words just spilled onto the page.

Doesn't that sound great? Perhaps you are sitting there, wondering how to make your story fit within a specific publishing house's guidelines, wondering if you can finish it before someone else steals your niche. Wouldn't it be nice not to wonder at all? Wouldn't it be great to just sit down and tell the story you want to tell? To write for the sheer joy of writing?

So what if ... what if you decide to take a different path instead? To write for the joy of it instead for what sells. After years of trying to follow market trends, I've chosen to take the different road. I'm writing the story of my heart. And let me tell you, friends, I welcome having the joy of writing back in my life.

What led to this change of heart? Well, for starters, I didn't finish the last two books I began. I tried, I really did, but my heart wasn't in them.

The characters didn't really speak to me. I felt as if I was only going through the motions. I was writing because it was my job and I was supposed to write, not because it was something I wanted to do.

Then, I got laid up for months with a bad disc in my neck. Lying in bed for weeks staring at the ceiling gives a gal plenty of time to think about what's missing from her life. I recalled how, once, at an RWA chapter meeting, a speaker asked us to sum up what writing meant to us in one sentence. I wrote, "Writing is joy."

But as I lay there counting ceiling tiles, I realized writing to me had become one big knot of frustration and anxiety instead.

I missed that joy... the feeling of excitement I'd once had as I brought a story to life. I missed having my characters speak to me. I missed the feeling of being unable to wait to write that next page.

What could I do to bring back the joy?

I had to write the story in my heart. So that's exactly what I started to do.

It's a story I've thought about for years. I used to tell it to myself as I went to sleep each night. But I never tried to write it because I knew it was a story that wouldn't sell. It doesn't really fit a specific niche. It crosses genres. It's a big story ... a long story... a complicated story.

A story that seemed impossible to pitch in a neat synopsis for an editor's desk.

Well, I thought, it wouldn't hurt me to write up few notes, would it? So one day I brought my laptop to bed with me and started writing an outline. Within an hour, I had over twenty pages of notes. Within an hour, I realized this was not one book, but a series.

I knew it was a series that might never sell, but that was the chance I was willing to take. Because it felt like the story of my heart. The story I'd waited a lifetime to tell.

I looked at it this way: even if the print houses didn't share my enthusiasm for it, there were always other paths with e-publishing, web publishing, or self-publishing. With so many options available these days, my story might find an audience after all.

Was taking the risk successful? Well, yes, I happy to say for me it was. The first book in this series, *Destiny's Dreamers*, was accepted by Awe-Struck E-books for release in Spring 2004.

Do I recommend this to others? I do believe it's worth examining why it is that we choose to write. To become famous? To get rich?

Or perhaps to tell a story that we really care about.

If you have reached the point where you've lost the joy of writing, maybe all you need to do is look inside your heart. It might not hold the key to your success, but it could hold the key to your happiness.

Section 6

Author Interviews

CHAPTER 42

A Conversation with Lorraine Heath

BESTSELLING AUTHOR LORRAINE HEATH has won numerous writing awards, including the 1997 RITA Award for Best Short Historical, the 1997 Holt Medallion for *Always to Remember*, and the 1995-96 Romantic Times Career Achievement Award for Americana Historicals for *Parting Gifts*. She has a B.A. in psychology from the University of Texas.

Lorraine is active in her local RWA chapter and often speaks at libraries and writers' conferences. You can visit her website at http://www.lorraineheath.com/index.html.

Rebecca Vinyard: You've recently added Young Adult romances to your book list. What made you decide to try that field? Do you find it more or less challenging to write than adult romance?

Lorraine Heath: I've met and and received e-mails from young ladies who read my adult romances. Because the books have adult content, I'm always a little uncomfortable recommending my books to younger readers. So I thought it would be fun to write a story with this younger audience in mind.

I find writing the stories equally as challenging as writing for an adult audience. I want to give the younger readers an emotional read. Yet, at the same time, I try to write a story that they can relate to. The world of a younger person is different from that of an older person. There is more of an innocence to it. So I try to capture that innocence in the story.

What is important to a younger person also is different. A younger person cares more about clothes than paying the utility bills and so my focus is a little different.

Vinyard: How are you able to create such believable characters? Their emotions always ring so true.

Heath: I think much of my success with creating believable characters stems from my interest in what makes people behave as they do. I have a degree in psychology, and I find people to be fascinating. Especially those who go about their daily lives, never bringing attention to themselves: the man you see every morning picking up his daily newspaper and you have no idea that he stormed the beaches at Normandy; the woman who checks you out at the grocery store and you don't ever realize she fought and won her battle against cancer.

I enjoy determining where people find their inner strength, why they behave as they do, creating heroes and heroines in the most common of situations.

Vinyard: Since you are also the editor for *The Rock*, an online e-zine by Painted Rock, and are active in your local RWA chapter, is it hard to set a schedule for your writing time?

Heath: After I sold my first book, I spent 7 years working another full-time job, so scheduling time to write became second nature.

I also discovered during this time that the more I had to do, the more I got done. If I have 10 pages to write and 8 hours to write them in—then I'll write 10 pages in 8 hours. If I have 10 pages to write . . . plus an article to write for *The Rock*, and a press release to send out for my chapter within an 8-hour period . . . then I do them all within that 8 hours.

I have a tendency to adjust the intensity with which I work based upon the amount of time that I have to work.

I've also found that doing small tasks such as editing *The Rock* or doing things for my chapter give me a sense of accomplishment—a small reward when writing a book takes awhile to accomplish. In other words, finishing the smaller goals keeps me going while I'm working to complete the larger goal.

Vinyard: You've won various awards, including Romantic Times Career Achievement Award. And you've been a *USA Today* bestselling author. Out of all your achievements, what did you find the most satisfying?

Heath: I'd have to say that I find the most satisfying to be that I've been married 26 years to my first husband and have two remarkable sons. As far as writing achievements, I would say receiving the RITA, the Romance Writers of America's most prestigious award.

Vinyard: Which of your books is closest to your heart? What made it special?

Heath: I believe every story I've written possesses something special, but *Always to Remember* is probably closest to my heart. I became obsessed with the story of a conscientious objector during the Civil War. I would write thirty or forty pages during one sitting. It was a story that required me to delve deeply into all the characters, which is something I enjoy doing.

I was challenged into making the characters sympathetic and at the same time justifying their questionable actions.

It was a very emotional book, and when I was finished writing it, I experienced a deep sense of satisfaction.

CHAPTER 43

A Conversation with Susan Elizabeth Phillips

In 2001, *New York Times* bestseller Susan Elizabeth Phillips was inducted into Romance Writers of America Hall of Fame. Other awards for Ms. Phillips include: RITA Awards for *First Lady*, *Dream a Little Dream*, and *Nobody's Baby But Mine*; RWA Top Ten Favorite Book Awards for *Breathing Room* and *Dream a Little Dream*, and the Romantic Times Career Achievement Award for *Kiss an Angel*.

You can visit her website at: http://susanelizabethphillips.com.

Rebecca Vinyard: Tell us about your first sale. I understand it is quite the Cinderella story.

Susan Elizabeth Phillips: In 1976, my husband's job took us from Ohio to central New Jersey. My best friend Claire lived two doors down the street. Both of us were big readers, reading everything from literary fiction to the newly popular historical romance novels. We loved talking about books—what we liked, what we didn't.

One day, just for fun, we decided to try to write a book together.

For three weeks, as we rode our bikes in the evening, with my toddler in the baby seat behind me, we plotted our story. Then we sat down with a yellow pad and began to write.

Four hours later, we'd come up with exactly *three* sentences. We had no idea how to write a book together, but we were getting a good idea how *not* to do it.

Over the course of the next few months, we worked out a system. We'd get together to plot a scene, frequently role-playing the dialogue. Claire would take copious notes, carry them to her typewriter, and come up with a rough draft, which she'd give to me.

Sometimes I'd just change a sentence here or there. Other times, I'd throw out all of her hard work and start over again. Somehow our friendship survived.

With only half the manuscript completed, we got the phone number of an editor at Dell Publishing. Sweating bullets, we called her. She was a very nice woman, asked us some questions about our book, and then agreed to see it, even though it wasn't finished.

Unfortunately, she also wanted to see a synopsis. *Synopsis?*

We barely knew what was going to happen in the next chapter, let alone the end of the book. Knees trembling, we ran to the typewriter and came up with something, then spent the next few weeks typing a fresh copy of our manuscript to mail off.

Three weeks later, the telephone rang. It was the editor. "I'm calling from Dell Publishing. We've read your manuscript. We like it. And Dell is prepared to make you an offer."

I never tell this story at writers' luncheons for fear I'll have to duck flying French rolls thrown by an angry audience. It sounds so easy. But the market was red hot then, and publishers were hungry for books. Unfortunately, it's not so easy now.

Vinyard: The settings and characters for your stories seem so vivid. Is it difficult for you to write such realistic descriptions?

Phillips: Everything about writing is difficult for me. I'm an intuitive writer, so I have no outline when I start, which makes the process fairly miserable sometimes. My favorite moments are when the characters whisper in my ear and write their own dialogue. If only it happened more frequently!

Vinyard: What did you do to celebrate the first time you made the *New York Times* bestseller list?

Phillips: The first time I made "the list," I was clueless about its importance. This was with one of my early books, *Fancy Pants.*

When I made the list again many years later with *Dream a Little Dream,* I celebrated with a little screaming and dancing around the room.

Vinyard: Tell us about your good writing days. And the bad ones! Do you write on a schedule?

Phillips: I'm very slow. And I have to travel quite a bit. So I generally try to work a full five-day week, eight o'clock to four-ish. I also try to write at least a little on Saturday and Sunday so I don't lose the flow.

Mornings are my best time. One of my favorite tricks is to hop out of bed, brush my teeth, and hop right back in again with my laptop. This way I can sometimes get an hour's work in before hunger and the distractions of the day drive me back out from under the covers.

Vinyard: Is any of your stories closer to your heart than the others?

Phillips: Whichever book I've just finished is always my favorite.

CHAPTER 44

A Conversation with Connie Flynn

CONNIE FLYNN is the bestselling author of ten novels in various romance subgenres including romantic suspense, romantic comedy and paranormal. Her books include *Shadow on the Moon, Shadow of the Wolf, The Fire Opal*, and *The Dragon Hour*.

She has conducted classes on novel writing at her local community college and has given programs at various writers' conferences across the United States.

You may visit her website at http://www.connieflynn.com.

Rebecca Vinyard: What made you decide to switch from writing category romance to paranormal?

Connie Flynn: I've always been a big fan of paranormal. At various times, I've wanted to be Dean Koontz, Stephen King, or Anne Rice when I grew up. So when the paranormal market opened up, it was natural for me to try my hand. I was so, so pleased when I sold my first book.

And I'm grateful that the market is opening up even more these days.

Vinyard: What role does research and pre-writing play in creating your stories?

Flynn: Early on, I had an editor tell me my "research was showing." And I realized the danger of knowing too much about a subject. So I'm not a fan of research and tend to do it on the fly as I write.

For technical details, I go to the children's library where complicated concepts are explained in simple terms. For day-to-day life, I go for the face-to-face interview and seek insider slang and acronyms to give the flavor of reality.

My series background taught me the value of the detailed synopsis. I have sold on less developed proposals—and found myself in rewrite hell as I wrote the story. So I returned to the basics.

But no matter how solid an outline is, it's no substitute for the actual writing. Lately, I've found that I tend to write until the flow gets stuck. At that point, I go back to my previous pages, examine the scenes, and expand, edit, move, or delete as needed.

But it took me a long time to work out this process. And it will probably change in the future, maybe book by book.

Vinyard: You're very good at creating tormented characters. Do you ever feel guilty for being so mean to them?

Flynn: Gosh, I'm going to have to reveal I'm a terrible person—but no. I give my characters the means to transform their lives, to better know who they are, and to win the partner they were fated to have. The rewards are high and relief is in sight.

I liken it to having them run a marathon. Or a baby. When it's all over, the results are so worth the pain . . .

Vinyard: What do you believe is the most important element of believable paranormal fiction?

Flynn: Creating a believable normal world with meticulous and relevant details, then doing the same in the paranormal world. The para-world must have rules and the writer must stay faithful to those rules and justify any deviations.

This is where Stephen King excels and why he stays on top year after year.

Vinyard: Which of your characters is closest to your heart?

Flynn: Lily DeLaVega, the fallen werewolf queen of *Shadow of the Wolf*. Lily was such a strong-willed and complex villain in *Shadow on the Moon* that I felt compelled to redeem her.

She was not your traditional innocent and well-meaning heroine. She came from a different world with different values and was forced by the hero Tony Whitehawk to come to terms with her own sins and her own humanity.

I doubt she was my readers' favorite character, but, to me, she rose to the challenge so beautifully that she won my heart. And those of the other characters in the story.

CHAPTER 45

A Conversation with Katherine Sutcliffe

KATHERINE SUTCLIFFE is a multi-award winning *USA Today* national and international bestselling author of twenty-two historical and contemporary suspense novels. She also has worked in the past as consultant head writer for the daytime dramas *As the World Turns* and *Another World*.

Her first foray into romantic suspense, *Darkling I Listen*, won numerous romantic suspense awards. Books currently in release include *Bad Moon Rising*, *Lover Beware* (co-author) and *Evil Rises*, all from Berkeley/Jove, and *Obsession* from Pocket Books.

Visit her website at http://www.katherinesutcliffe.net.

Rebecca Vinyard: Why did you switch from writing historical romance to romantic suspense?

Katherine Sutcliffe: I had been writing historicals for nearly twenty years and I felt I was running out of juice. Not only that, my writing has always had a darker spin to it and, generally, more plot than your typical romance.

I had wanted to try my hand at writing contemporary suspense for nearly ten years. Alas, my publisher kept saying no. "If it ain't broke, don't fix it." It wasn't until Christine Zika moved over to Jove from Dell that my dream came to fruition.

Christine knew me from my Avon days, had followed my writing long after I left Avon, and she suspected that, because of my darker, more complex writing, that I should be allowed to give it a shot.

She really stuck her neck out for me by convincing the publisher that my writing style would lend itself to contemporary suspense. Fortunately, *Darkling* was very successful.

Vinyard: Do you find writing contemporary stories more or less challenging than historicals?

Sutcliffe: Far less challenging, but oh, so much more fun! First, I can call on my own experiences more. I can better relate to the characters.

Research is vastly less challenging, and the same is true for writing dialogue. I don't have to sweat so much over each word in an attempt to make it sound as if someone in 1800s England is saying it.

Vinyard: What was it like working as a consultant head writer for daytime television?

Sutcliffe: Writing for daytime television was one of the highpoints of my career. It was very exciting to see my stories come to life on the television screen.

But I must admit, it was the hardest work I've ever done. As head writer, I had to come up with the six-month storylines. I also had to oversee the five "breakdown" writers, to make certain they were staying on course. Alas, the six-month storylines were frequently having to be changed. Perhaps an actor's contract wasn't renewed. Or they quit. Or someone got pregnant. And so on. So the document was in a constant state of rewriting.

Then there were the bi-monthly trips to NYC for ten-hour meetings, during which we had phone conferences with the head of daytime television on the West Coast. Not to mention the occasional eight-hour phone conferences when I couldn't be in NYC. I put in fifteen-hour work days, seven days a week.

Obviously, my book writing was put on hold, and this job certainly made me appreciate the advantages of being a novelist. When I was offered a two-year contract to move to NYC and take over the position of head writer for *Another World*, I did think long and hard about it . . . but said, "Thanks, but no thanks."

And returned to the serenity of book writing.

Vinyard: For me, *Darkling I Listen* was a wonderful story. It broke one of the many "rules" writers often are given, since the hero was an actor. Do you feel it is a mistake for new writers to write by the rules instead of writing the story in their hearts? Or should a new writer follow the rules—until they are in a position when they can break them?

Sutcliffe: The trick is how to write your story in a way that it *manipulates* the rules to your benefit.

Yes, Brandon Carlyle was an actor. However—and this is a big however—Brandon was removed from Hollywood and plunked into a small East Texas town. Therefore, we avoided the glitz and glamour of Tinsel Town. Which, in my opinion, is what the publishers want to avoid—that particular lifestyle—as opposed to the "actor" as a character himself.

Asking me about breaking the rules? In my opinion, rules are made to be broken. However, the writer must weave a good enough story to justify the breaking of the rules. If the book is well written, compelling, and powerful, "rules" don't apply.

Unless you get into controversial political or religious aspects. Go that route, and the writer is going to hit some major walls.

Vinyard: Which of your books is closest to your heart? What made it special?

Sutcliffe: That book would be *Darkling I Listen*. I returned to my East Texas small town roots. Been there, done it, seen it. Much of Alyson James's past was developed around my own childhood.

But, more importantly, this book allowed me the freedom, at long last, to do my thing without the normal genre restrictions that too often cramped my creativity, not to mention my writing style.

CHAPTER 46

A Conversation with Judy Christenberry

I N 2002, Judy Christenberry won the National Reader's Choice Award (Best Traditional) for *Newborn Daddy*. She has written over seventy books for Harlequin/Silhouette's various imprints, making her one of the leading voices in category romance today.

Rebecca Vinyard: Have you ever considered writing single title?

Judy Christenberry: Actually, I've written two single title books, one for Harlequin and one for Silhouette. The first one, *Unbreakable Bonds*, was part of the Randall series. The second one, *Hush*, part of the Circle K series, is to be released in Fall 2003.

But I'm also working on a stand-alone single title. Right now it's titled *I Shot the Sheriff*. My agent has looked at it, and I hope to redo a proposal and have it out on the market soon.

Vinyard: Do you have any new series in the works?

Christenberry: My Randall series is ongoing. And my next Tots for Texans will be ready in May to celebrate Harlequin American Romance's 20th year.

And I'll have two books out this Fall in the Circle K series. But I intend to start another series, to begin with a novella out in January 2004. The tentative flash is *Gathering the Berrys*, about a woman adopted as a baby who discovers she has siblings out there somewhere.

I love connecting books.

Vinyard: You have dozens of books on your backlist, with eight releases last year alone. What's your secret to being such a prolific writer?

Christenberry: Motivation! I have expensive children! Actually, I enjoy being in the middle of a story. I'm not sure why I have so many stories to tell, but I pray I never run out of them.

I wanted to quit teaching school, which required more books to replace that income. I stopped teaching in 1996. And I've been writing nonstop since them.

Vinyard: Your stories are so funny and fast-paced, without resorting to a lot of sex and violence. Would you say put a lot of yourself into your books?

Christenberry: Believe it or not, when I first tried to write contemporaries, my heroine cried a lot. Debra Matteucci saw something she liked in that first book—and taught me to do a better job.

What readers admire is a heroine who can face difficulties with courage and a smile.

And yes, part of me is in every book. I don't know how to write any other way.

Vinyard: What do you think about people who say category romance is nothing but babies, cowboys, and brides?

Christenberry: When someone says category is only about cowboys, babies and brides, I say, "And you have a problem with that?"

Seriously, those elements are popular for good reason. A cowboy represents the white knight in shining armor. He's an honorable man who works outdoors, close to nature, who appreciates life, women and children. At least mine are.

Babies represent the coming together of a man and a woman, a new beginning.

Brides are women poised on the verge of change, true love, and building a new life.

There are other hooks, but those are three good ones. Romance writers are savvy writers. We start a story where there's action.

My daughter was trying to read a popular mainstream author. She said that the first 40 pages showed poor writing and seemed to have no relevance to anything. So she put it down.

Now, forty pages in a romance—you're *way* into the story.

CHAPTER 47

A Conversation with Suzanne Brockmann

SUZANNE BROCKMANN has won the Romance Writers of America's favorite book of year three times in succession, for the years 2000, 2001, and 2002. Her other awards include the RITA, the Holt Medallion, and fifteen Wish awards from *Romantic Times*, as well as a career achievement award for series romance.

She currently has had thirty-four books published, with multiple new releases and reprints scheduled for coming seasons.

Rebecca Vinyard: My father was a thirty-year Navy man. And I enjoy the authenticity of your Navy Seals. How much research went into creating your Troubleshooter series?

Suzanne Brockmann: Thank you for that compliment. The answer is—a lot! And the research is always ongoing . There's so much I don't know about the U.S. Navy, having never served in the military.

Well, okay, except for that short stint in the Civil Air Patrol when I was 13, but I don't think that counts!

My research really started back when I was eleven years old, when I read every book on my public library's shelves about WWII. I read everything from dry strategic breakdowns of individual battles to exciting true-life adventures like *The Great Escape*.

Because of all that military nonfiction I've read (and loved!) throughout my life, I had a really terrific foundation of understanding and respect for the men and women who serve our country in the armed forces.

And, oh, it's been such a *struggle* to do all that research about Special Ops. I'm kidding! I'm fascinated by the SEALs, and I'm always looking to read and learn more.

The most difficult thing, however, has been getting up-to-date info on the SEAL teams. There are lots of books available about Vietnam era SEAL operations. But more recent activities are classified, though. And rightly so.

In addition to research from books, television (the Discovery Channel has some great programs on the SEALs) and online, I've also visited the UDT/SEAL Museum in Ft. Pierce, Florida. It's a great source of information, and a truly wonderful museum.

Vinyard: In light of today's political climate, do you find it difficult writing fiction about the military?

Brockmann: Absolutely not! My various characters and I may or may not share the same political views, but that's okay. I'm writing fiction. My job is to make my characters as well-rounded and believable as possible.

As a writer, I don't have to believe *what* they believe, I simply have to understand *why* they believe what they believe . . . to make them ring true.

Vinyard: I know you've done you've done workshops on creating believable characters. What do you feel is the key to creating one?

Brockmann: For me, the key to creating believable characters lies in understanding them—knowing them well enough to throw them into any situation and let them react believably.

Good characterization, I feel, comes from *showing* the reader who the character is through his or her reaction to action. In other words, through the plot.

Vinyard: You've written for category lines, series, and single-title books. Which do you prefer, and why?

Brockmann: To be honest, I love variety. And I love a challenge. I enjoy writing everything, including television scripts and screenplays.

But my absolute favorite thing to write is a book that both stands alone and yet is part of an ongoing series. Like my current Troubleshooters series for Ballantine. I love returning to a familiar world, to familiar characters. It's like hanging out with good friends.

Vinyard: What advice would you give a new writer?

Brockmann: Read! And pay attention to your reaction to these books as a reader. Learn to analyze every piece of fiction you read. Or see—there's a lot to learn from television and movies, too!

Don't just study the books you loved, but really take apart the books that didn't appeal to you, too. Try to figure out exactly where the author lost you as a reader.

And with the books you loved, try to figure out what the author did to hook you. Where exactly did you fall in love with the hero? What made you unable to put the book down even though it was 12:30 at night and you had to be up at 6:00?

I've found that I can learn something about storytelling and writing from every piece of fiction that I encounter.

Section 7

Resources for Authors

CHAPTER 48

Mass Market Publishers

Avalon Books

Thomas Bouregy & Co., Inc.
160 Madison Avenue
New York, NY 10016
(212) 598-0222
(212) 979-1862 FAX
editorial@avalonbooks.com
www.avalonbooks.com

Editorial Director: Erin Cartwright
Editor: Mira S. Park

Publishes the following categories: career romance, general romance, historical romance, mystery, and western. The career and general romances are contemporary; all westerns are historical. Length: ranges from a minimum of 45,000 words to a maximum of 60,000 words.

Submission guidelines
Include the following with your submission:

- Query letter addressed to: The Editors

- Synopsis (2-3 pages.)

- First three chapters

- A self-addressed, stamped envelope (SASE) *or* note in your query letter that you do not want the partial returned.

- Accepts unagented work and multiple submissions. Indicate if it is a multiple submission in your query letter.

Avon

10 E. 53rd St.
New York, New York 10022
212-207-7000
avonromance@harpercollins.com

Executive Editors: Carrie Feron, Lucia Macro
Senior Editor: Lyssa Keusch
Editor: Erika Tsang
Assistant Editor: Kelly Harms
Editorial Assistant: Selena Mc Lemoru

Seeking romances in three particular areas: historical romance; contemporary romance, including romantic suspense; and African-American romance, trade paperback women's fiction.

Historical Romance
Avon Romance, Avon Treasure, and Avon Superleader. (100,000 words, approximately 400 pages)

These are love stories set primarily in Great Britain and the United States before 1900.

Contemporary Romance
(100,000 words/approximately 400 pages)

Seeks stories of emotional complexity, written by authors with unique voices. Books with humor, drama, romantic suspense.

"All types and tones can be right for Avon. If your manuscript is exciting, electrifying, and exceptional, then we want to see it."

African-American Romance
(90,000 words/approximately 380 pages)

Actively seeking romance with African-American heroes and heroines. These should be contemporary love stories of approximately 90,000-100,000 words, set in the United States.

Submission guidelines

To submit historical or contemporary romance, query first. Your query should be brief, no more than a two-page description of your book. Do not send chapters or a full synopsis.

Please e-mail your query to avonromance@harpercollins.com.

INTERVIEW WITH EXECUTIVE EDITOR
Lucia Macro
Avon

RV: According to *Publishers Weekly*, Avon has been encouraging their authors to create worlds with reoccurring casts of characters. Does this mean Avon is shifting its focus into series romance?

Macro: I think that we've encouraged authors to build worlds when the authors come to us with a good idea. It's not an active shift into series romance. We take everything on a case-by-case basis. Is it right for the author? Is it right for her characters? Is it right for her book? It really depends on those factors. We work with each author individually and this trend does not reflect a corporate shifting in any major way.

RV: What do you feel is the most common mistake new authors make?

Macro: Sometimes new authors do everything right, and then we buy the book and it is published. When we decline a manuscript, there's usually not a single common reason. Sometimes it's that the writing is not up to snuff. Sometimes it's the characters just aren't coming alive. Sometimes the dialogue is stilted. There are unfortunately a lot of different things that can go wrong with a manuscript.

RV: Do you have any particular kinds of stories on your wish list?

Macro: I would never want to say Avon looks for specific types of stories or that they always want a certain type of book. I think what we do is judge each book and each author individually. We're just looking for authors who have a high level of creativity, have a wonderful voice, and are able to tell their story in a vivid and fascinating and wonderful and romantic way.

And that's what we're really looking for rather than any specific type of story. As editors we have to keep our fingers on the pulse of the marketplace. In many cases the market dictates what's most popular and what's not working. That can ebb and flow, so we're constantly looking for all different kinds of stories.

RV: Avon was the first company to give contemporary romance covers an innovative fresh new look. In light of this, do you feel the classic clinch covers will eventually disappear?

Macro: I see no signs that the classic clinch cover is going to disappear simply because there are a lot people out there who like them. I think there's a segment of the marketplace that looks for them. They like to look at the characters and see what they are doing and what they look like and where the book is set.

So do I think it will disappear completely? No.

Ballantine/Ivy

1745 Broadway
New York, NY 10019
Phone: 212-782-9000
FAX: 212-940-7500
Web site: www.ballantinebooks.com

Editorial Director: Linda Marrow
Editor: Charlotte Herscher
Editorial Assistant: Adriana Nova

Highly selective; publishes a relatively small list.

Submission guidelines
No published guidelines available. Unagented writers should query first.
Then, send 50 pages, synopsis, and SASE if the editors request to see
more of your work.

The Bantam Dell Publishing Group

1540 Broadway
New York, NY 10036
Phone: 212-782-9000
Web site: www.bantamdell.com

Senior Editor: Wendy McCurdy
Executive Editor: Jackie Cantor
Assistant Editor: Anne Bohner
Assistant Editor: Abby Zidel
Assistant Editor: Elizabeth Scheier

Submission guidelines
Currently accepting only agented material. Unagented material will be

returned unopened. Does not accept unsolicited manuscripts, e-mail submissions, or material printed on dot-matrix printers.

Barbour Publishing, Inc. and Heartsong Presents

PO Box 719
Uhrichsville, OH 44683
Web site: www.barbourpublishing.com/

Fiction Editor: Rebecca Germany

Heartsong Presents considers inspirational contemporary and historical manuscripts between 45,000 and 53,000 words.

The underlying theme in Heartsong Presents' romances is the belief that a true and honest faith in God is the foundation for any romantic relationship. The love between a man and a woman is the key ingredient of every Heartsong Presents inspirational romance. It should be obvious why the hero and heroine love each other, and their love should be realistically developed with God as the center.

Current need: Looking for stories with an ethnic flavor and are also interested in stories that have a seasonal theme. The theme of a season or holiday can be woven throughout or be a part of a major scene in the book.

Submission guidelines
Send a 2-3 page summary of the story along with 3-4 randomly selected chapters, plus return postage, to:

Heartsong Presents
Rebecca Germany, Fiction Editor
PO Box 719
Uhrichsville, OH 44683

Berkley/Jove

375 Hudson Street
New York, NY 10014
212- 366-2000
www.penguinputnam.com

Senior Editor: Gail Fortune
Senior Editor: Christine Zika
Senior Editor: Allison McCabe
Senior Editor: Kim Lionetti
Senior Editor: Cindy Hwang

Description: Publishes historical romance and contemporary romance under the Jove and Berkley imprints.

Submission guidelines
For guidelines, send SASE.

Dorchester Publishing/Leisure Books/Love Spell

200 Madison Ave., Suite 2000
New York, NY 10016
212-725-8811
Web site: http://www.dorchesterpub.com

Vice President, Editorial: Alicia Condon
Senior Editor: Chris Keeslar
Editor: Kate Seaver
Editorial Assistant: Micaela Bombard

All Romances are approximately 90,000-100,000 words and in the following categories: Historical, Futuristic, Time-travel romance, Paranormal romance, Contemporary romance

Submission guidelines

Please query first, or submit submit synopsis and first three chapters only. Do not send complete manuscripts unless specifically requested to do so. Prefers manuscripts written from the third-person point-of-view. Include a stamped, self-addressed envelope for possible return of proposal or manuscript. No material will be returned without SASE.

Genesis Press

315 Third Avenue North
Columbus, MS 39701
662-329-9927
Web site: www.genesis-press.com/

Editor: Nyani Colum

Romance imprints include: Indigo, Indigo Vibe, Love Spectrum, and Erotic Romance.

Characters must be African-American or multi-cultural. Erotica by women for women. Unlike mainstream erotica, Indigo After Dark is art, not porn, and prefers its characters not to be portrayed as such.

Submission guidelines

Query with first three chapters and a brief synopsis (no more than five pages). We will request full manuscripts (80,000 to 100,000 words) only after examining the synopsis and first three chapters.

Harlequin / Harlequin Mills & Boon / Mira / Silhouette / Steeple Hill

Toronto
Harlequin Books, MIRA Books
225 Duncan Mill Road
Don Mills, Ontario
M3B 3K9
Canada
416-445-5860

Marsha Zinberg, Senior Editor, Special Projects
Brigit Davis-Todd, Executive Editor, Blaze
Paula Eykelhof, Executive Editor, American Romance
Laura Shin, Senior Editor, Superromance
Brenda Chin, Associate Senior Editor, Temptation
Wanda Ottewell, Editor Duets
Dianne Moggy, Editorial Director, MIRA Books

Imprints include: Temptation, Duets, Blaze, Harlequin Superromance

New York
Silhouette Books, Harlequin Books, Steeple Hill Books
233 Broadway, Suite 1001, 10th Floor
New York, NY 10279
Phone: (212) 553-4200

Tara Gavin, Editorial Director
Leslie Wainger, Executive Senior Editor, Suspense and Adventure
Karen Taylor Richman, Senior Editor, Silhouette Special Edition
Marie-Theresa Hussey, Executive Editor, 'Tender'
Tracey Farrell, Executive Editor, Harlequin/Silhouette Single Titles
Denise O' Sullivan, Senior Editor, Harlequin Intrigue
Melissa Endlich, Associate Editor, Harlequin Historicals

Imprints include: Harlequin American, Harlequin Intrigue, Silhouette

Bombshell, Silhouette Intimate Moments, Silhouette Desire, Steeple Hill Love Inspired

London

Harlequin Mills & Boon Ltd.
Eton House, 18-24 Paradise Road
Richmond, Surrey
United Kingdom
TW9 1SR

Web site: http://www.eharlequin.com/

Karin Stocker, Editorial Director
Tessa Shapcott, Senior Editor Presents
Linda Fildew, Senior Editor, Historical Romance
Shelia Hodgson, Senior Editor Medical Romance
Samantha Bell, Senior Editor, Romance and Red Dress Ink

Imprints include: Harlequin Presents, Harlequin Romance

Submission guidelines

Unless otherwise noted in specific guidelines for a given program, do not send unsolicited complete or partial manuscripts. Instead, submit a query letter first, with SASE. The query letter should include word count and publishing credits. Also include a synopsis (no more than two single-spaced pages).

Harlequin, Silhouette, Mills & Boon, and Steeple Hill publish only category/series romance (and inspirational romance under Steeple Hill). Please do not submit any other type of fiction or nonfiction.

Your manuscript should be told in the third person, primarily from the heroine's point of view. Please see the guidelines for each series for details.

Multiple submissions are not acceptable; do not send any material that is being considered by another publisher. A literary agent is not required in order to submit.

You must enclose a SASE with all material you send in. Please send an envelope large enough to accommodate your work, plus adequate postage (in the form of international postage coupons or an international money order, where appropriate).

INTERVIEW WITH EXECUTIVE EDITOR
Leslie Wainger
Harlequin New York

RV: Tell us a bit about yourself and your position at Harlequin. What is your average work day like?

Wainger: As the executive editor for the Suspense and Adventure category, I oversee Silhouette Intimate Moments, Harlequin Intrigue and the upcoming Silhouette Bombshell line. I also function as the senior editor for SIM, while Denise O'Sullivan is the senior editor for HI and Lynda Curnyn is associate senior editor for SB.

In my role overseeing the category, I'm looking at big-picture issues and strategizing for all three lines' success in the marketplace, to make sure we present the highest quality suspense- and adventure-oriented romance while still maintaining different editorial positionings to satisfy the maximum number of readers.

For SIM specifically, I handle all the acquisition decisions, as well as scheduling and copy, and have a hand in cover development.

Finally, I also handle an author base of both series and MIRA writers, so I've never lost touch with what brought me to this business in the first place.

RV: What do you feel makes Harlequin's books unique?

Wainger: Series romance provides a haven for readers, a place where a woman can go with the assurance of finding the right romance to satisfy her. Whether it's sensual or traditional, short and straightforward, or complex and even suspenseful, she can be certain of finding both high quality and a happy ending. I don't know of any other publisher that can offer such an array of romances for every taste on an ongoing basis.

Harlequin/Silhouette really is synonymous with both romance and quality, which is a testament to the talent of our authors, of course. And that, too, is something we can do—in my opinion, anyway—better than anyone. We find and develop amazing writers, and allow them to tell all kinds of stories and get them to the readers on a timely schedule.

RV: What do you feel is the most common misconception about category romance?

Wainger: That there's a formula for writing it. Certainly there are reader expectations, but readers of any genre fiction—mystery, science fiction, thrillers—also have expectations, and there's not a thing wrong with that.

Another major misconception is that the books are all the same, though even perusing the back cover copy for any given month can dispel that one. Lastly, it makes me crazy when people insist the books are ground out by talentless hacks. Nothing could be farther from the truth; just see my comment above about author development, or think about the number of major and bestselling authors who got their start in series romance.

RV: What are the most common mistakes new authors make?

Wainger: Thinking it's going to be easy and quick to write a book. Thinking her heart doesn't have to be in it. Trust me, the readers always know when an author's faking it. Forgetting how crucial the building blocks—pacing, tension, strong and individualized characters—are; no plot is clever enough to make up for the lack of the basics.

And every author needs to find and trust her own voice. That, more than anything, is what keeps a reader coming back for more.

RV: Can you tell us something about Harlequin's new lines? For example, you've introduced a fantasy line that does not emphasize romance.

Wainger: The person to talk to about Luna, our new fantasy line, is Mary Theresa Hussey, one of my fellow executive editors.

Silhouette Bombshell, a 4-book-per-month line, launches in July 2004. The books are very heroine-focused and action-oriented. Romance is a secondary concern. While the romance will go to the next level at the end of the book, that could simply mean a first kiss.

The real focus is the strong, kickass heroine, a woman who's got power and knows how to wield it. Saving the world from nuclear destruction is not beyond her capabilities, though she may also operate on a less international or large-scale canvas.

We do have guidelines available for writers, and we're all actively looking for new authors who can handle that line's challenges.

ImaJinn Books

PO Box 545
Canon City, CO 81215-0545
877-625-3592
Web site: http://imajinnbooks.com/

Senior Editor: Linda Kichline

Publishes supernatural, paranormal, fantasy, futuristic, and time-travel romances. Length: 70,000 to 90,000 words.

Submission guidelines

ImaJinn recommends that you either check their website, or e-mail or write to see what types of books they're currently seeking. The company only considers queries with story lines that meet current needs.

You do not need an agent to submit, but you must query first. All query letters should include a synopsis no longer than six double-spaced pages; it may be submitted by regular mail or e-mail.

If you mail your query, please include an SASE.

Kensington Publishing Corp.

850 Third Ave.
New York, NY 10022
212-407-1500
Web site: http://www.kensingtonbooks.com/

Editor-In-Chief: Michaela Hamilton
Editorial Director: John Sconamiglio
Editorial Director: Karen Thomas
Editorial Director: Kate Duffy
Executive Editor: Ann LaFarge
Editor: Hilary Sares

Imprints include: Arabesque, Brava, Zebra, and Regencies. Publishes contemporary and historical romance, regencies, and women's mainstream fiction.

Submission guidelines

Unsolicited material is accepted for Arabesque, Brava, and Regencies only. Send cover letter and a synopsis (3-5 pages), with first three chapters, and SASE if you need your material returned.

Arabesque: Multicultural romances, 80,000-100,000 words. Write to Karen Thomas for guidelines.

Brava: Erotic Romance, Contemporary and Historical, 100,000 words novels, 25,000-30,000 words novellas. Submit to Kate Duffy.

Regencies: 75,000 words.

New American Library (NAL) / Penguin Putnam (USA) Inc.

375 Hudson Street
New York, NY 10014
212-366-2000
Web site: http://www.penguinputnam.com/

Editorial Director: Claire Zion
Executive Editor: Audrey LeFehr
Executive Editor: Ellen Edwards
Associate Executive Editor: Hilary Ross
Senior Editor: Laura Cifelli

Imprints include: Signet, Onyx, and Accent. Publishes historical romance under Signet and "mainstream" contemporary romance and women's fiction under Signet, Onyx, and Accent.

Submission guidelines

Prefers agented writers, but will consider a manuscript if it has a strong query letter. Include SASE and address a specific editor. No unsolicited e-mail queries or manuscripts are accepted.

Submit regencies to Hilary Ross, historical and contemporaries to all editors.

Pocket Books

1230 Avenue of the Americas
New York, NY 10020
212- 698-7000
Web site: http://www.simonsays.com/

Editorial Director: Maggie Crawford
Senior Editor: Amy Pierpont
Senior Editor: Micki Nuding

Editor: Lauren McKenna
Associate Editor: Christina Boys
Assistant Editor: Selena James
Assistant Editor: Deirdre Dore

Publishes single title historicals, contemporary romance, romantic suspense, women's fiction trade paperbacks, gothic, and paranormal romances.

Submission guidelines
Send query letter and SASE. Will accept unsolicited manuscripts, partials with synopsis, unagented writers and multiple submissions.

Red Sage Publishing, Inc.

PO Box 4844
Seminole, FL 33775
727-391-3847
Web site: www.redsagepub.com

Editor: Alexandria Kendall

Publishes romance novellas, 25,000 to 35,000 words. Stories should focus on main characters' relationship, strong emotional and physical conflict.

Submission guidelines
Query with one-page synopsis and first ten pages.

St. Martin's Press

175 Fifth Avenue
New York, NY 10010
212-674-5151
Web site: http://www.stmartins.com/

Executive Editor: Jennifer Enderlin
Editor: Monique Patterson
Assistant Editor: Kim Cardascia

Publishes contemporary romance, historical romance, romantic suspense and paranormal.

Submission guidelines

No unsolicited manuscripts. Queries accepted. No unagented authors unless material is solicited.

Tor/Forge

Tom Doherty Associates, LLC
175 Fifth Avenue
New York, NY 10010
212-388-0100
Web site: www.tor.com

Senior Editor: Melissa Ann Singer
Senior Editor: Natalia Aponte
Senior Editor: Claire Eddy
Assistant Editor: Anna Genoese

Publishes historical, paranormal, horror, SF/Fantasy, and time travel with romantic elements. Plot elements and character development must be equally strong.

Submission guidelines

Submit first three chapters and synopsis. Full submission guidelines available on web site.

Submit horror and mysteries to Melissa Ann Singer, mysteries and suspense to Natalia Aponte, historicals, horror, and SF/Fantasy to Claire Eddy.

Submit paranormal romances to Anna Genoese. Specific guidelines for this program are located at: http://www.tor.com/paranormalromance.html.

Heartquest/Tyndale House Publishers Inc.

351 Executive Drive
Carol Stream, IL 60188
630-668-8300
Website: http://www.heartquest.com

Editor: Anne Goldsmith

Publishes novellas and series novels. Novellas, 25,000 words. Novels, 75,000-100,000. Stories must have strong Christian elements.

Submission guidelines

Write for guidelines before submitting.

Warner Books

Time and Life Building
1271 Avenue of the Americas
New York, NY 10020
212-522-7200
Web site: http://www.twbookmark.com/romance/index.html

Editorial Director: Beth de Guzman

Senior Editor: Karen Kosztolnyik
Editorial Assistant: Michelle Bidelspach
Editorial Assistant: Melanie Murray

Publishes single title historical and contemporary romances, romantic suspense, women's fiction and paranormal romance, but not time travel.

Submission guidelines

Agented submissions preferred, but query letters will be reviewed as time allows. No unsolicited manuscripts or proposals.

CHAPTER 49

Electronic and Small Press Publishers

Awe Struck E-Books

http://www.awe-struck.net
Genres Published: Romance: all subgenres except inspirational, Science
Fiction, Historical fiction, Ennoble Series (features heroes/heroines who
are disabled).

DiskUs Publishing

http://www.diskuspublishing.com
Genres published: Romance (all categories) Science Fiction, Fantasy,
Horror, Mystery, Western, Children's and Young Adult novels.

Double Dragon Publishing

http://double-dragon-ebooks.com/
Publishes all genres, including romance

Ellora's Cave Romantica Publishing

http://www.ellorascave.com
Publishers category length (40,000 words) and novella-sized 'romantica' fiction in both e-book and print formats. Looking for stories with strong sexual content. Submission guidelines can be found on site.

Fiction Works

http://www.fictionworks.com
Genres published: Fiction: Fantasy, Historical Fiction, Horror, Inspirational, Mainstream, Mystery, Romance, Science Fiction, Western, Young Adult. Nonfiction: Business titles, How-to, Self Help.

Hard Shell Word Factory

http://hardshell.com
Genres Published: Romance, Mystery, Science Fiction and Fantasy, Western and Historical, New Thought and Nonfiction, Children and Young Adult.

Lion Hearted Publishing

http://www.lionhearted.com/
Publishes e-books and trade paperbacks. Contemporary and Historical Romance.

LTD Books

http://www.ltdbooks.com/
Canadian e-publisher specializing in all genres of fiction except erotica.

New Concepts Publishing

http://www.newconceptspublishing.com/
Genres published: Romance (all subgenres), Mystery, Science Fiction, Fantasy, Horror, Young Adult.

Novel Books Inc.

http://www.novelbooksinc.com
Publishes romance, mystery, horror, science fiction, fantasy

RFI West

http://www.rfiwest.com/
Formerly Starlight Writers, Dark Star, and Pulsar Books. Publishes all genres, except erotica and children's books.

Treble Heart Books

http://www.trebleheartbooks.com/
Romance genres, Mystery, nonfiction. Includes former MountainView Publishing as a division.

Wings ePress Inc.

http://www.wings-press.com/
Romance genres, Young Adult, Mainstream, Mystery, Science Fiction, Light Horror

CHAPTER 50

Books & Websites for Authors

Books On Writing

The Artist's Way: A Spiritual Path to Higher Creativity
by Julia Cameron and Mark Bryan
Julia Cameron and Mark Bryan lead you through a comprehensive twelve-week program to recover your creativity from a variety of blocks, including, fear, jealousy, guilt, and other inhibiting forces, and replace them with artistic confidence and productivity.

Bird by Bird
by Anne Lamott
Inspirational book that discusses everything from writer's block to creating characters and plots, and writing dialogue.

The Character Naming Sourcebook
by Sherrilyn Kenyon, Hal Blythe, Charlie Sweet
Out of all my reference books, this one is my favorite. This is a dictio-

nary of names and their meanings, categorized by ethnic origin. There are also essays explaining the importance and usage of names for characters, settings and objects; as well as conventional usage within the various fiction genres.

The Complete Writer's Guide to Heroes and Heroines
by Tami D. Cowden, Caro LaFever, Sue Viders
This book specifically identifies character archetypes including descriptions of specific qualities, flaws, background, and occupations.

Dangerous Men, Adventurous Women:
Romance Writers On The Appeal of Romance
by Jayne Ann Krentz (editor)
Bestselling romance novelists take on the myths and misconceptions about the romance genre in this collection of essays.

Getting the Words Right: How to Rewrite, Edit and Revise
by Theodore A. Rees Cheney
This book discusses how to revise your work to make it clear and concise.

Goal, Motivation, Conflict: The Building Blocks of Good Fiction
by Debra Dixon
This book takes a writer through the process of creating believable plots and characters use a step by step approach. A must have book for every writer.

The Romance Writers' Phrase Book
by Jean Salter Kent
An excellent source to help break through narrative blocks and describe your story's action. It has hundreds of phrases, some hilarious when taken out of context, but all designed to help get you get your story moving.

The Writer's Journey: Mythic Structure for Writers
by Christopher Vogler
Discusses how plot and characters in successful fiction follows the basic structure set forth in myths. Vogler takes the writer step by step through the hero's journey as seen in myths and movies.

Writing Down the Bones: Freeing the Writer Within
by Natalie Goldberg.
This inspirational book teaches you how to build up your writing skills gradually, just as a runner trains to run a marathon.

Writing Romances: A Handbook by the Romance Writers of America
by Rita Gallagher (Editor), Rita Clay Estrada (Editor)
A collection of essays written by a variety of bestselling romance authors. Each essay highlights a specific and vital area of writing or publishing your romance fiction.

Essential Reference Books

Bartlett's Roget's Thesaurus

Bartlett's Book of Love Quotations
by Barbara Ann Kipfer (Compiler), John Bartlett

Elements of Style
by William Strunk, Jr., E. B. White

Webster's Dictionary of American English

Websites for Writers

Association of Authors' Representatives
Great place to start an agent search.
http://www.aar-online.org/

Bartleby.com
The online version of *Bartlett's Quotations* can be found at: http://www.bartleby.com/100; and there is an online version of Strunk and White's *The Elements of Style* at http://www.bartleby.com/strunk.

eHarlequin.com
Harlequin's web site includes submission information and a special section for writers.
http://www.eharlequin.com/cms/index.jhtml

The Literary Times
Online version of the romance writer and reader magazine, including how-to articles on writing.
http://www.tlt.com

The Passionate Pen
Excellent site with articles on writing, agent and romance publishers information.
http://www.passionatepen.com/index.htm

Preditors and Editors
Information and recommendations on publishers and agents.
http://www.anotherealm.com/prededitors/

Romance Central
Workshops, information, and resources for romance writers.
http://romance-central.com

Romance Writers of America
Up-to-date information on RWA National, as well as local chapter information.
http://www.rwanational.org/

Romantic Times Online
Online version of the popular romance writer and reader magazine.
http://www.romantictimes.com/

Slake
The perfect place for romance writers to find reviews, quotes, and information.
http://www.slake.com/

Subversion: Celebrating Women's Fiction
Must-see site with author interviews and articles on writing.
http://www.booksquare.com/subversion/index.cfm

The Word Museum
Excellent articles on fiction writing, also reviews, classes, and author sites.
http://www.wordmuseum.com

Audio Tapes

Romance Writers of America members can buy audio tapes of the programs held at the yearly national conference as well as find tapes from some local chapters. Contact RWA for more information.

Contributors

Rosalyn Alsobrook

Award-winning author Rosalyn Alsobrook has had over 29 books published. Her many awards include the prestigious Romance Writer's of America's Lifetime Achievement Award for 1999. Visit her on the web at: http://home.earthlink.net/~ralsobrook.

Shelley Bradley

Historical romance author Shelley Bradley is a former Golden Heart finalist and past president of the North Texas Chapter of Romance Writers of America. Her books include *Strictly Forbidden* and *Strictly Seduction*, *One Wicked Night*, as well as the Brothers-In-Arms medieval trilogy. Visit her web site at: http://shelleybradley.com.

Liz Flaherty

Liz Flaherty has had two books published, and she's hard at work on other projects. Married for thirty-some years to Duane, her own personal hero, and mother of three and grandmother of five, Liz also works a day job. She plans to retire as soon as she finds the time. Visit her website at http://lizflaherty.romance-central.com.

Connie Flynn

Connie Flynn's novels span the romance sub-genres of paranormal, romantic suspense, and humor. Her paranormal novels have consistently hit online bestseller lists, and her book *The Dragon Hour* won RWA's FF&P Chapter's Prism Award for best time-travel romance. She has taught romance writing classes, and now offers intensive one-day workshops where she shares the writing tools she's picked up on her writer's journey. Visit her website at: http://connieflynn.com.

Sharon Ihle

Sharon Ihle is the bestselling author of a dozen award-winning historical romances set in the American West. Visit her on the web at: http://romance-central.com/SharonIhle.

Dovie Jacoby

Born under lucky stars on October 24th in the distant past, and raised in Dallas, Texas, as the youngest of four girls and dozens of cousins, there seemed to be no early indication that Dovie would become a writer. The muse struck her in her mid-thirties, and she was compelled to write, beginning by writing four fantasy books plus several short stories and poems. Dovie also writes book reviews for Romance Central.

Rene Miller Knudsen

Rene Miller Knudsen has written one historical novel and is currently working on two others. She graduated with honors from the University of California at Santa Cruz with a degree in history.

Caro LaFever

Caro LaFever is a founding member of Heart of Denver Romance Writers. Her long contemporary, "Night Dreams," was a 2000 Golden Heart finalist. Her nonfiction book, *The Complete Writer's Guide for Heroes and Heroines* (published by Lone Eagle), co-written with Tami Cowden and Sue Vider, was also released in 2000.

Patricia McLinn

Patricia McLinn is a bestselling and award-winning author of category romance, longtime journalist, and a winner of the Romance Writers of America's Veritas Award. She has had over twenty books published. You can visit her on the web at: http://www.PatriciaMcLinn.com.

Rachelle Morgan

Rachelle Morgan has received a number of award nominations for her eight historical romances published by Avon Romance and Berkley Publishing. Visit her on the web at www.rachellemorgan.com.

Ruth Scofield

Ruth Scofield is a Missouri native who lives with her beloved husband and hero, Charles. Her world consists of her family, friends, writing, and her faith. Her inspirational novels include love in its greatest tests and a strong faith in God. Besides inspirational novels, she writes Americana westerns. Her first was a RITA finalist. She has won the Holt Medallion and been a finalist twice. Ruth often speaks to schools and libraries about writing and publishing. She is a member of Romance Writers of America, Heartland Romance Authors, Novelists, Inc., and The Author's Guild. Her website is: http://ruthscofield.romance-central.com.

Rebecca Vinyard

Rebecca Vinyard, a former journalism major and e-zine editor, is a member of the Dallas chapter of the Romance Writers of America. She is also the webmaster of Romance Central, a site serving romance writers, which can be found at http://romance-central.com. She has been published in fiction, series fiction, nonfiction, and poetry.

Rebecca Wade

A transplanted Californian, Rebecca Wade has lived in Germany, the West Indies, and Australia. During her years abroad, her lifelong love of reading developed into a passion for writing. She is the author of three historical romance novels for Avon Books. Currently, she lives in Texas with her husband, her daughter, and two sleepy black-and-white cats. . Visit her website at: http://www.dhc.net/~wade.

Index

The Writer

The Writer was founded in 1887 by two reporters from the *Boston Globe*. Their mission was to create a publication that would be "helpful, interesting, and instructive to all literary workers." The magazine soon became an essential resource for writers, publishing articles in the first half of the 20th century by literary luminaries such as William Carlos Williams, Wallace Stegner, Sinclair Lewis, William Saroyan, Daphne du Maurier, and many others.

After a long editorial tenure into the latter half of the 20th century by A. S. Burack and then Sylvia K. Burack, in the year 2000 Kalmbach Publishing Co. purchased the magazine, along with its affiliated line of books on writing fiction and nonfiction, and moved the editorial operations from Boston to Waukesha, Wisconsin (a suburb of Milwaukee).

Continuing its long heritage of more than 110 years of service, *The Writer* continues to be an essential resource for writers into the 21st century, providing advice from our most prominent writers, featuring informative articles about the art and the business of writing.

It is dedicated to helping and inspiring writers to succeed in their endeavors and to fostering a sense of community among writers everywhere.

More information on *The Writer,* with current articles and other resources, can be found online at the magazine's Web site, http://www.writermag.com.

—Elfrieda Abbe, Editor
The Writer